The Nenets' Song

For Yuri

The Nenets' Song

A Microcosm of a Vanishing Culture

ALLA ABRAMOVICH-GOMON

Routledge
Taylor & Francis Group
LONDON AND NEW YORK

First published 1999 by Ashgate Publishing

Reissued 2018 by Routledge
2 Park Square, Milton Park, Abingdon, Oxon, OX14 4RN
711 Third Avenue, New York, NY I 0017, USA

Routledge is an imprint of the Taylor & Francis Group, an informa business

Copyright © Alla Abramovich-Gomon, 1999

The author has asserted her moral right under the Copyright, Designs and Patents Act, 1988, to be identified as the author of this work.

All rights reserved. No part of this book may be reprinted or reproduced or utilised in any form or by any electronic, mechanical, or other means, now known or hereafter invented, including photocopying and recording, or in any information storage or retrieval system, without permission in writing from the publishers.

Notice:
Product or corporate names may be trademarks or registered trademarks, and are used only for identification and explanation without intent to infringe.

Publisher's Note
The publisher has gone to great lengths to ensure the quality of this reprint but points out that some imperfections in the original copies may be apparent.

Disclaimer
The publisher has made every effort to trace copyright holders and welcomes correspondence from those they have been unable to contact.

A Library of Congress record exists under LC control number: 99063690

ISBN 13: 978-1-138-33662-9 (hbk)
ISBN 13: 978-1-138-33663-6 (pbk)
ISBN 13: 978-0-429-44293-3 (ebk)

Contents

Ashgate Studies in Ethnomusicology General Editor's Preface

The aim of this series is to encourage ethnomusicological study (with 'ethnomusicology' defined very widely), which has significance for all those involved in it. The series is interested in work which emphasizes the relationships between people and music in cultural context, as individuals within communities, and which acknowledges a varied range of contributions and looks to beneficial outcomes for those 'being researched' as well as for the 'researcher'. To this end it supports what might be regarded as a dialogic praxis, of collaborative discursive action and reflection, in which the researcher might become part of the facilitation of a particular focus, in time and place. It is also an intention to enable the investigation and problematizing of ethnomusicological practices, and to discuss ways of clarifying such issues and addressing them.

There is a place in the series for the 'traditional' studies of particular musical practices, where these are related to cultural and functional significance, and where they give an insight into modes of representation and transmission. This is particularly true where the research process gives those sharing the information a new and useful view of their own activities. Innovative and experimental work that is appropriate to the principal aims of the series is also encouraged.

Malcolm Floyd

King Alfred's University College, Winchester

List of Maps and Plates

Maps

Plates

Between pages 82 and 83

List of Figures and Music Examples

Figures

Music examples

Preface and Acknowledgements

When I started thinking about music as a musicologist, I began to appreciate old folk song traditions as an invaluable source of knowledge about the roots and basics of music. In the 1970s, this scholarly interest drove me to the Nenets tundra in search of comparative material to add to my previously conducted research on the music of Finno-Ugrian peoples. Since the fieldwork, I have been continuously exploring the theoretical tools necessary for the scientific explanation of the musical phenomena. This book has brought together the results of both efforts: the discovery of the music and the discovery of its interpretation. As such, it has also fulfilled my obligation towards many people.

The Nenets singers are the first on this list, and I hope that I have managed to attract attention to the musical talent of this nation.

By carrying this study through, I have paid my debt to Zinaida Kupriianova, Natalia Tereshchenko, and Galina Grachiova, scholars who dedicated their entire lives to the study of Arctic peoples and their cultures. I had an opportunity to meet Zinaida Kupriianova and Natalia Tereshchenko at their apartments in Leningrad some time after I returned from my trips to the Nenets tundra and shortly before incurable diseases took their lives. Both of them acknowledged the need for musicological studies of the Nenets' song. Galina Grachiova visited me in 1990, at my home in Indianapolis, when she came to work at the Eiteljorg Museum on the Smithsonian Institute's exhibit dedicated to the Arctic peoples. Soon after her visit, I learned about the crash of a helicopter carrying Russian ethnographers to the Arctic. Galina Grachiova was among those who died in that crash. I was left with the memory of our last conversation about the changing political situation in Russia, and the Nenets' music. The courage, dedication and commitment to research exemplified by these three outstanding women motivated me to bring my work on the Nenets' song to completion despite numerous obstacles.

I would like to express my gratitude to Dr Izaly I. Zemtsovsky, the former head of the Folklore Department at the Russian Institute for the History of the Arts, Russian Academy of Science, St Petersburg (currently, a Visiting Scholar at the Center for Slavic and East European Studies at the University of California, Berkeley), and to the late Dr Boris N. Putilov, the Senior

Scholar of the Museum of Anthropology and Ethnography, Russian Academy of Science, St Petersburg. These two leading Russian folklorists promoted my work on the Nenets' song during the time when my family, continuously refused permission to emigrate from the former Soviet Union, was struggling with a difficult life situation.

In the United States, I was encouraged by Professor Gyula Décsy from the Uralic and Altaic Studies Institute at Indiana University, Bloomington, to continue my study of the Nenets' song.

I am very thankful to Bruno Nettl, Emeritus Professor of the University of Illinois at Urbana-Champaign, who took the role of my major adviser when I decided to present the work as a PhD thesis. Entitled 'The Nenets Song Tradition', the thesis was completed in 1996.

Ain Haas, Professor of Sociology at Indiana University Purdue University of Indianapolis (IUPUI), and my colleague at the Earth Music Center of Indiana (EMCI), became involved in the later revision of this work. I am thankful to him for always being available when I need advice on the subtleties of English.

I would like to acknowledge the input of the librarians who helped me obtain many hard-to-find sources that are included here as references: Barbara Howes at Butler University, Indianapolis; Kari Jahr and Matthew Radican at IUPUI, Indianapolis; Dr Moira Smith at the Indiana University, Bloomington; and Julia Gauchman at the University of Illinois at Urbana-Champaign. Suzanne G. Snyder, Production Editor of Macmillan Publishing USA, helped me submit the manuscript on time by compiling the index.

I am especially grateful to Rachel Lynch, Commissioning Editor at Ashgate Publishing, for her thorough editing of the submitted manuscript, and to the other Ashgate editors, Ruth Peters and Caroline Cornish, for their guidance during the production of the book.

Finally, I would like to thank my husband, the principal supporter of all my professional endeavours.

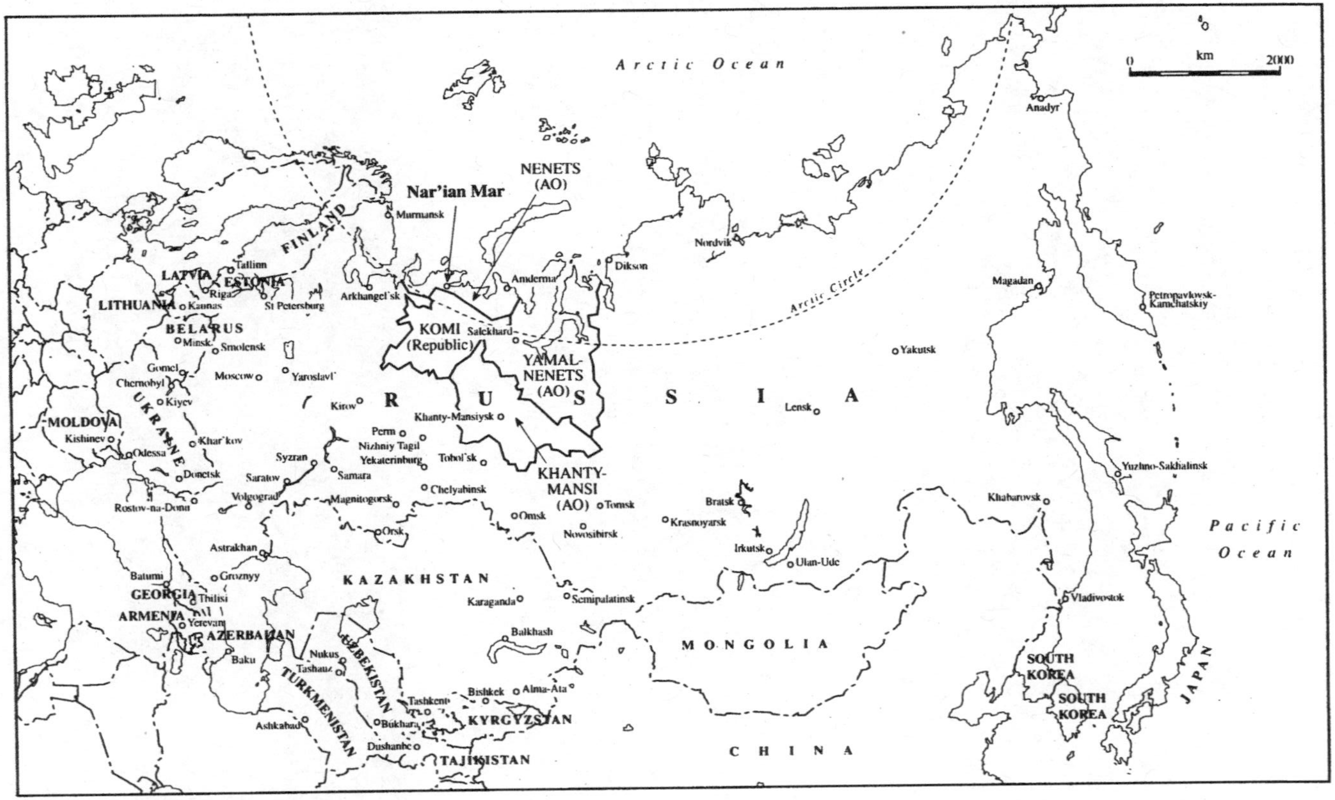

Map showing territory inhabited by the Nenets

Introduction

... the mind gathers the resembling ideas together into one conception.[1]

This book examines the oral song tradition of the Nenets people, one of the twenty-six northern minority nations of the former Soviet Union, now Russia. The Nenets live along the Russian coast of the Arctic Ocean in a tundra land characterized by its monotonous plain landscape and scanty vegetation. Their territory includes the adjacent European and Asian parts of the tundra (see map on p. xiii).

Many abrupt and fundamental changes have taken place in the Nenets' land, economy, and social structure in the course of this century. Before 1920, the people lived in a nomadic clan-based society, kept reindeer herds, and observed a shamanistic religion. In the early 1920s, the Soviet State government formed after the Great October Revolution of 1917 began an imposed reorganization of the Nenets' traditional culture in accordance with a socialistic pattern of a sedentary village community, a collective farm economy, and a communist ideology.

The Nenets' song tradition has survived this transition. Still an integral part of the everyday life of the people, it faces unprecedented new challenges to its existence. The collapse of the Soviet Union in the early 1990s has opened up opportunities for the global economy to spread into the Arctic region. Full of unexplored natural resources, the land is now attracting international business enterprises (Specter, 1994: 7, 12). It seems unlikely that the Nenets' song tradition will remain unaffected for long by western popular culture accompanying these economic changes.

For the present, however, the genuine native song tradition endures. As in earlier centuries, the songs are still passed on by word of mouth, and their musical style remains intact. This makes them unusual today, when, as a result of the globalization process, most forms of music are 'crossovers', 'hybrids', or 'mixes' of styles and traditions, and when a question has been raised: 'Where can we find traditional music that remains uninfluenced by any culture but its own?' (Hall, 1991: 38). The Nenets' song offers an answer. It survives as a surprising rarity, bearing not a single trace of Western influence.

An important feature of the Nenets' song tradition is its essentially epic character, which is a testimony to the fact that at the turn of the twenty-first century, 'epic regions inhabited by epic peoples' (Hatto, 1981: 13) still have a place on the map of the world. The Nenets' song tradition is one of these musical 'oases'. It has survived in Northern Eurasia, the land of well-known heroic epics such as Finnish *Kalevala* and Yakut *Olonkho*.

A long time ago, almost all peoples in the world performed epic songs. Intrigued by the universal impulse of human beings to sing long stories about their experiences of the world, scholars have tried to locate as many different manifestations of the epic phenomenon as possible for comparative purposes. The International London Seminar on Epic (ILSE) was organized with this goal in view. The findings of the seminar, active during 1964-72, were summarized in a collection of essays in which the Nenets' epic tradition was mentioned only briefly (Hatto, 1981: 18-19). One of the aims of this study is to demonstrate that the Nenets' tradition deserves to be recognized on a par with other epic treasures.

The ILSE developed a classification system for epic song traditions. Three, very loosely defined, categories of tradition were identified: (1) purely oral traditions involving oral composition-performance and oral transmission of songs; (2) sub-oral traditions combining the usage of printed song texts with the traditional oral style of performance; and (3) post-oral, 'secondary epics' utilizing written means of composition and transmission, and preserving only some of the traditional stylistic features.

The Nenets' tradition of epic song falls under the first category of purely oral artistic phenomena. This largely illiterate 'epic people' could hardly take advantage of the song text transcriptions published by scholar-collectors.

The extinction of the Nenets' traditional religious and social institutions, which had in various ways been connected with the performance of song, and the aging of the singing population, were the reasons why Soviet folklorists predicted the rapid disappearance of the Nenets' song. They called for a collection and archival preservation of the songs perceived as a 'rescue operation'. Not only the Nenets' but all other oral traditions in North-Eurasia have been seen in this light, yet many of those traditions have continued to exist despite the prognoses of their immediate extinction. The disappearance of the Karelian lament tradition, for example, had been anticipated long before the late 1960s and early 1970s, when I had the opportunity to observe a funeral ritual in a Karelian village, performed according to all traditional norms, with the complete cycle of the ritual laments sung by professional lamentors, and with listeners of all ages participating in the ritual. Similar ceremonies involving the entire village communities routinely took place in the Russian North among Russian, Karelian, Vepsian, Izhor, and Komi peoples.

I discovered the same discrepancy between scholarly expectation and actual reality in respect to the Nenets' song tradition. In 1965, Zinaida Kupriianova expressed an opinion that Nenets epic songs were on the brink of disappearing. She wrote in the introduction to her publication of the songs that the young generation of Nenets would only be able to learn their national songs from books (Kupriianova, 1965: 56). However, when I arrived a decade later at the same settlement Kupriianova had visited, I found that almost every person in the settlement knew and could perform repertories of the songs. Moreover, there were a number of bards who were masters of song improvisation and whose talents were widely recognized by the people themselves. Far from moribund, the tradition remained intact, unaffected by modern means of composition or transmission, despite the changes taking place around it. Although all the singers were adults of different ages, I saw young people and children among the listeners. No wonder that a new, educated generation of native performers has now emerged, who are passing the tradition on to various audiences, including analysts and researchers.[2]

According to the recent information on the state of the Nenets' song tradition, vocal performances remain a fixed part of the people's life. In 1994, Finnish ethnomusicologist Jarkko Niemi visited the same Nenets settlement which I had visited almost twenty years previously. He told me that although he had not found the same singers I had worked with in the 1970s, he had met many other excellent performers. Obviously, the pessimistic predictions of the songs' fast decline were proved false by the Nenets themselves.

Until there is just one talented, or merely skilful, performer capable of singing an epic song remaining, the prognoses of the end of the performance tradition of these songs are premature. They are true only to the extent that death does end the creative thoughts of individuals. Yet the life of the entire song tradition cannot be measured by individual lives. Culture has its own life, overlapping with but far exceeding the lives of its numerous messengers. Living people carry on the memories and performing skills, even if the routes and rules of the tradition change. They revitalize the collective knowledge and live it through their performances over and over again.

Such an understanding is consistent with an anthropological theory of experience formulated in the early 1980s by Victor Turner (Bruner, 1986). Unlike the preservationist tradition in folklore discipline, associating the performances with the past, the theory highlights the significance of their existence in the present. The concept of experience (*Erlebnis*, or 'lived through') focuses on the individual who, by engaging in performance, re-experiences a culture, filtering it through his/her consciousness. Every individual performer revives a cultural tradition, encapsulates the experience of others, and re-creates, re-tells, re-constructs, and re-fashions the tradition (Bruner, 1986: 3-30). The observable emergent qualities of performance are in the musical behaviour and the manner of performance of an individual singer, in his/her interaction with audience, and in the environment of performance in general. They are of interest to both the folklorist studying artistic performance in the light of culture and the anthropologist studying culture in the light of performance.

As for the study of epic song traditions, it is as important to keep an eye on the past as on the present. The concept of tradition, by its definition, implies the existence of the past in the present. In this regard, the role of ethnographic observation is to look for the remnants of the past in the present performance environment, in order to find out in what way epic traditions are 'expressive of their mother-cultures' (Hatto, 1981: 10).

But what if the performance practice outlives its 'mother-culture' and exists today in a completely changed social environment? How can we learn about the traditional culture, if there is not much left from the past to observe? In this case, in addition to the method of field observation centered on the present situation and the emergent individual qualities of performance behaviour, we can draw upon the method of reconstructive ethnography, which targets the substance of performance, the structural system of the song tradition which might have symbolized vanished, no longer observable social and cultural phenomena.

If the musical style of performances remains strictly traditional, it can't be considered only an emergent aspect of performance. Having emerged long ago, this style has no relation with the present other than through some novelties of the performers' interpretation, or the emergent character of performance behaviour and performer/audience interaction. Stored in the memory of the performers, and reproduced by them in accordance with certain rules developed in the culture and society which no longer exist, it is, on the contrary, a stable and predetermined aspect of performance. As a remnant of the vanished culture, the traditional musical style carries invaluable information about the environment which shaped and influenced it. Reconstructions of the historical contexts of musical systems fruitfully complement field observations of performance events. The combination of the two methods of musical investigation helps to determine both independencies and interconnections, 'gulfs as well as bridges' (Geertz, 1966: 66) in the music/culture correlation.

In 1970s, at the time of my fieldwork, the Nenets' epic tradition occupied a relatively independent gulf-space in the society, established on the ruins of the destroyed traditional society. As the people kept it safely, within the private space of their life, the tradition remained stylistically indifferent to the new social orders and customs. This private (as opposed to officially institutionalized) status of the epic tradition secured the interconnections and bridges the latter had built with the old shamanistic culture, thus creating an analytical opportunity for us to restore those bridges. Such a restoration becomes a part of this study. Revealing the role of the songs in the past, it aims to enhance our understanding of the songs in the present.

The retrospective contextual analyses of the Nenets' song is possible due to the efforts of many specialists in various areas of ethno-science, who managed to describe the traditional culture of the northern peoples at the time when it was available for observation. Scholars investigating the Arctic and Siberian regions accumulated a substantial amount of evidence that could be relied upon in the restoration of the Nenets' culture from its song. The restoration involves testing the accumulated ideas by musical evidence, and vice versa.

A synthesis of the Nenets' musical data with the existing scope of ethnographic data has never been undertaken before. All musical studies of this song tradition have lacked a consideration of the music through the prism of its culture. Because authors have dealt only with musical transcriptions and textual analyses of the songs' recordings, the role of the songs in the Nenets' culture could not be brought to light. It is the major goal of this study to remedy this oversight, and bring the melodic system of the songs under the scrutiny of various contextual analyses.

The retrospective contextual analysis of epic song traditions has its advantages. Shaped by their cultures and societies, the melodic systems of the traditions constitute unique resources of knowledge about these two larger phenomena, and awareness of the connections between musical systems and their traditional cultures and societies allows us to understand what makes a particular epic tradition different from other similar traditions. Scholars have come to realize that their concern with universal qualities of epic traditions disguises the uniqueness of each tradition: 'When I think of epics,' said Arthur Waley, 'I think how different they all are' (Hatto, 1981: 1). They have called for special attention to individual qualities of the traditions, each presenting an idiosyncratic case in terms of 'experiences of their societies', and a 'latent potential of their languages' (1981: 2-3). The 'latent potential' of musical creativity is not mentioned in these arguments, yet nobody seems to question the fact that musical styles of national epics do determine both the uniqueness and universality of the epic traditions.

Since epic song is originally and essentially a musical phenomenon, inquiring into the origin of its musical qualities becomes indispensable for its more or less adequate understanding.

We initially experience the uniqueness of a musical tradition when listening to performances in their natural settings, yet we arrive at the place with certain expectations based on our previous experiences. It is natural to start looking for the things that we know similar musical traditions have, and we may feel slightly disappointed after discovering that these familiar things are in fact missing. It takes a while to overcome prejudices and to realize that whatever this particular musical culture is lacking compared to other cultures forms a part of its uniqueness.

The Nenets' musical reality is striking given the lack of many musical practices which exist in other cultures. The people do not dance nor do they play instruments. They sing only solo rather than in choir or ensemble. They do not have canonical folklore genres accompanying the rites of passage, and they do not like discussing their songs, preferring singing to talking about it. Their sole aim as musicians is to sing stories about their heroes and themselves, and they are amazingly good at it.

Following the simplest principle of musical composition – a constant reiteration of a concise melody – they explore the potential of seemingly limited means of musical expression. They are able to use their voices as an instrument splitting, sometimes, into two hidden melodic lines. They provide each melody with a unique rhythmic design, letting the melodic intonations follow the emotional 'ascents' which they often have during song improvisations. By means of basically one and the same musical form, which sustains endless substitutions of plots and contents, they manage to accommodate different performance occasions and life situations.

Thus, the musical culture observable in the life of the Nenets is confined to an exclusively vocal soloist tradition of which the major form has been song with predominantly epic genre characteristics. The exclusively vocal character of the Nenets' musical tradition relegates it to the group of similar traditions lacking insrumental performances (Key, 1963: 18), in contrast to those traditions in which 'vocal music is surprisingly unimportant' (Turino, 1989: 6).

The question may arise as to what extent this study, based on the fieldwork done among only the European part of the Nenets' population, can afford a level of generality implied by the concept of national tradition. The main factor justifying and securing this generalization is the typicality of my material, verified by recordings made at other Nenets locations. Many stylistic similarities found between the songs from various collections prove true the view expressed by the experts in Nenets ethnography that this culture, including all its domains, is extremely homogeneous. This has allowed me to understand the stylistic features of my collection of songs as pertaining to the national tradition. Of course, since this study is the first attempt to understand Nenets' song as a cultural phenomenon of the present and the past, future corrections and amendments to the observations and hypotheses presented here are inevitable.

Finally, I would like to comment on the theoretical aspect of the book. For the following interpretation of the Nenets' song the ethnomusicological principle of studying music *in* or *as* culture has been essential. I have combined this principle with my understanding of the music/culture relationship as an ingredient of a larger coherence envisioned by Charles Sanders Peirce (1839-1914). Peirce's concept of semiosis introduces a broader sphere of connections which includes the continuity between nature and culture. As it incorporates natural environment, economy, social structure, and human cognition and creativity into a uniform network of relationships, it directs us towards an understanding of the oneness of natural and cultural phenomena which grow, ramify, parallel, intertwine, and intimately depend on each other. Such an understanding is extremely appropriate for the study of the traditional culture of the Nenets people who consider nature inseparable from all human endeavours, and who worship it as an inexhaustible source of life and as superpower. Based on such fundamentals my goal has been to rediscover the coherence specifically manifesting itself through the interrelationship of music and culture. Turning to culture in order to explain music I also focus on music to explain culture, thus showing how the part and the whole furnish mutual explanations of one another.

The title of the book reflects the holistic approach. By naming the Nenets' song a microcosm of their vanishing culture I imply that song as a whole, as well as song melody alone, reveals important information about its 'mother-culture' and traditional society. Each single melody emerges embodying a larger universe, and the way the melody symbolizes different aspects of the whole can be as enlightening for understanding non-musical cultural phenomena as the knowledge of culture and society is to understanding the meaning of music.[3]

At more detailed levels of analysis I have followed the rule that the individual nature of empirical data determines the type of its analytical treatment, as well as dictating the focus of interpretation (Behague, 1984: 9). Searching for explanations to more specific problems, I have resorted to various methods of analysis and have utilized a diverse set of resources in the form of theoretical ideas which cut across different disciplines and theoretical camps. I have come to believe that such an eclectic theoretical approach to interpretation serves the process of increasing understanding of things better than loyalty to a single theory. The approach excludes the absolutism and isolationism innate to thinking within a closed theory, stimulates openness to the thoughts of the past and others, and allows more space and freedom for associations and analogies. There has never been and never can be an ideal theory, but any theory may contain fruitful ideas. Searching for corroborating ideas from different theoretical traditions may only benefit research. Therefore, I have tried various keys to this interpretation: from rediscovering dormant yet still vigorous thoughts hidden in the 'old-fashioned' volumes to testing the concepts and beliefs of the native people by contemporary scientific categories.

An inspiring example of such an approach to theoretical thinking is the scholarship of Roman Jakobson who favoured ideas from different traditions. I fully adhere to his *credo* that creative theoretical thought 'results from the concurrence of traditions, interdisciplinary outlooks, scholarly fellowship, and fidelity to one's own pursuits' (Waugh and Monville-Burston, 1990: 31).

Similar principles have been also propagated by Clifford Geertz, who thinks that looking 'beyond narrowly defined theoretical tradition' can stimulate theoretical advances. Although he stands out against 'solemn reduplication of the achievements of accepted masters' and the 'sweet sense of accomplishment which comes from parading habitual skills', he advises us not to abandon the established traditions but to widen them. Geertz sees 'no other road of escape from ... the dead hand of competence' than 'moving in different directions' (1966: 2).

Moving in various theoretical directions is natural when addressing unclarified problems. I faced a number of such problems: the controversial social situation of the Nenets' song performance practice marked by the dramatic conflict between the inner world of the singers and their alien socio-ideological environment; the intriguing introverted manner of performing behaviour that distinguishes some of the Nenets bards; the intimate connections between the almost destroyed traditional culture and the songs' structural system embodying that culture; the difficulties of analysing the multi-level complexity of song form; the native interpretive ideas and customs related to the song melodies – the association of the melodies with thought and brain, and the custom of personal ownership of the song melodies. It is the challenge of understanding these phenomena that led me beyond a 'single-handed' theoretical approach to interpretation (Herzfeld, 1993: 241).

One important point calls for reiteration: idiosyncrasies and multiple aspects of investigated phenomena put a demand on their theoretical interpretation to be flexible, diverse, and adjustable. This is true by virtue of the fact that any theoretical knowledge of culture is helpful yet inferior to a real knowledge of *a* culture. Umberto Eco's metaphor is a picturesque equivalent to this argument.

> If we put together many branches and great quantity of leaves, we still cannot understand the forest. But if we know how to walk through the forest of culture with our eyes open, confidently following numerous paths which criss-cross it, not only shall we be able to understand better the vastness and complexity of the forest, but we shall also be able to discover the nature of the leaves and branches of every single tree (Eco, 1990: xiii).

In terms of this analogy, what follows is my 'walk through the forest' of the Nenets' culture. The walk-interpretation is largely a subjective experience of gathering various ideas into one conception and applying them to the reality of the Nenets' song tradition. I expect the results of this experience to be improved by others interested in increasing our understanding of this thought-provoking subject.

Notes

1. Peirce, 1931, vol. 1: 365.
2. For example, the analyses of Nenets songs by Hajdu (1978) and Vakhitova (1988), are based on the performances of the two Nenets professionals: linguists Vasily Ledkov and Ielena Susoi respectively.
3. The assumed type of relationship between the part and the whole is analogous to the physical phenomenon of hologram found characteristic for perception and cognition. The essence of hologram is such an integration of elements within a system which allows each of the elements to contain and display the properties akin to the whole (Pribram, 1971: 140-66; Pietsch, 1981).

CHAPTER ONE

The People of the Tundra Land

> **Now, be the Owner of the Land!**
> **Feed your people unequally:**
> **Give some of them more,**
> **Some of them less.[1]**

The Nenets[2]

Geographical distribution, population, environment

The Nenets (also known as Yurac, Hasava, Samoyed) people live in the far north of the Russian Federation. They occupy a vast Arctic land of over 450,000 square miles stretching from the White Sea in the west to the Yenisei river in the east. The northernmost borders of their land reach the islands of the Arctic Ocean: Novaia Zemlia, Kolguiev, and Vaigach. The southern borders run across the basins of the Taiga rivers: the Polui, Nadym, Pur, and Taz. Some Nenets groups approach the neighbouring areas populated mainly by Russians (the North Dvina river near Archangel, and the Onega river). A small number of the Nenets reached the Kol'sky peninsula, the northern parts of the Komi Autonomous National District, and the Khanty-Mansi Autonomous National District.

The whole of Nenets territory consists of a few tundra areas: Kanin Tundra (the Kanin peninsula), Timan Tundra (from the Pesha river to the Indiga river), Malaia Zemlia (from the Indiga river to the Pechora river), Bol'shaia Zemlia (from the Pechora river to the Kara river), and Yamal Tundra (the Yamal peninsula). The tundras are organized into the administrative units of (1) the Nenets Autonomous National District (Archangel Province), with the capital Nar'ian Mar, and (2) the Yamal-Nenets Autonomous National District (Tiumen' Province), with the capital Salekhard (formerly Obdorsk).

Linguistically and culturally the Nenets are related to other inhabitants of the circumpolar area of Eurasia, known by the general name Samoyed: Sel'kup (Ostyak-Samoyed), the Nganasan (Tavgi-Samoyed), and the Enets (Yenisei-Samoyed). According to the census of 1989, there were 39,754 inhabitants of the Samoyed group in the country; 34,665 of this amount were the Nenets, who appeared to be the largest population among the Samoyed and other Northern Minorities of Russia (Vakhtin, 1994: 34).

The majority of the Nenets form a group referred to as the Tundra Nenets. The rest comprises a very small group (about 1200 people, according to the 1962 census) called the Forest Nenets. They live in a far eastern part of the Nenets territory in the taiga of the Pur River basin, which belongs to both Yamal-Nenets and Hanty-Mansi District. In the 19th century, as a result of mixed marriages between the Nenets and the Komi (the Finno-Ugrian people), a further group emerged called the Kolvin Nenets. Although the Kolvins speak the Komi-Izhem language, they consider themselves Nenets.

The Nenets of the European tundra are surrounded by Russians, who came to the Pomor'ie region in the middle of the 19th century, and the Komi, who moved to the north in the 16th century. A regular Nenets 'sovkhoz' (Soviet Farm) usually comprises a mixed population (Nenets, Russian, and Komi). On the Kol'sky peninsula the Nenets are surrounded by the Saami and the Russians, whereas in the east, in the Yamal Tundra, the Nenets' neighbours include fellow Samoyed peoples (the Enets and Nganasan), Finno-Ugrians (the Hanty and the Mansi), and other northern peoples (Kets, Evenks, and Dolgans). All these peoples share the severe living conditions of the Arctic climate, characterized by permafrost, long-lasting polar days and nights, long and cold winters, and short, cool summers.

Names and language

There are different hypotheses on the etymology of the term Samoyed referring to the Nenets and their linguistic and cultural relatives (Khomich, 1966: 24-7). For example, a partial answer has been suggested by P. Hajdu, who excludes the origin of the word from the Russian language (Hajdu, 1950: 6-18). The name Yurak as applied to the Nenets was thought to originate from the Nganasan, the Nenets' relatives and neighbours in the east, who used to call the Nenets of the Yenisei region by a similar name, *d'uraka*. M. Castren applied this name to all tundra Nenets, and scholars of the Finno-Ugrian and other Western traditions continued adhering to this term.

Today the people have chosen to call themselves Nenets. For this reason, they appear in this book under this rather than any other name. The name Nenets has been an official designation of these people since their inclusion in the former Soviet State. It is based on the word *nenei* meaning 'man', or 'real man', and *nenei ne* meaning a 'real woman'. It has been suggested that the people gave themselves this name when they began separating from other Samoyeds (Khomich, 1966: 24). As an ethnonym, 'Nenets' was already in use at the end of the 18th century (Georgi, 1799: 4). In everyday life, however, it is usually substituted by a clan name. Most of the last names of the people have been traced to a few clan names associated with the Siberian tundra area. Later, when the Nenets spread over the European tundra territories, those original clans formed new families acquiring new names (Verbov, 1939; Dolgikh, 1970a).

Besides a clan name individual Nenets have a variety of other names signifying their various identities. An individual may also have a taboo-name, nickname, common name-address, teasing name, official name (a Christian name in tsarist Russia and a passport name in the former Soviet Union and today's Russia), as well as a name after death (Pushkariova, 1990b: 141).

The Samoyed group of languages consists of the North and South Samoyed branches. The northern branch includes the most closely related languages: Nenets, Enets, and Nganasan. The southern group consists of Sel'kup and the languages of the Samoyed tribes of the Sayan mountains, which have now been almost completely assimilated by neighbouring Turkic people.

Among all the Finno-Ugrian languages it is the language of the Lapp that is most closely related to Samoyed. The Lapps live today in the Arctic parts of Scandinavia and Finland, but mainly on the Kola peninsula. Both the Samoyed and the Lapps are known to be the most ancient surviving inhabitants of the Arctic. The common roots of the two languages have been discussed in a number of comparative linguistic studies (Bubrikh, 1948; Toivonen, 1950; Collinder, 1954), which have also prompted various theories on the relations the Lapps and the Samoyeds may have with an aboriginal Arctic population (Tereshchenko, 1992: 52).

Linguists have been studying the Samoyed languages extensively since the 18th century (Sorokina, 1990: 66-71). They have detected two major dialects in Nenets: the Tundra and the Forest dialects, with further classification of the Tundra dialect into three groups: the West, the Central (Great) and the East. However, scholars admit that these dialects share a basically homogeneous structure, and that the differences between them have never been an obstacle to communication between the Nenets (Khomich, 1966: 24; Tereshchenko, 1990: 7).

Nenets has a very interesting structure. Among its most fascinating characteristics are a consonant phoneme *h* called a voiceless 'glottal stop'; the predestinative and predicative inflections, occurring between the stem and the equivalent suffix; objective conjugation, indication of the category of number (singular, dual, plural) both in nominal and verbal inflections; and 'a fantastic abundance of grammatical forms' (Décsy, 1966: 4). The language is also characterized by a vowel harmony, which is a particular form of limitation of vowel occurrence, and by avoidance of more than one consonant at the beginning of words. Nenets vocabulary incorporates older words borrowed from Turkic, Komi, Ob-Ugric languages, and about 1,500 new words adopted in the twentieth century from Russian (Décsy, 1966: 14, 15, 42).

Modern standard Nenets-Yurak was codified by Georgy Prokof'iev and his colleagues in the Institute of Northern Peoples in Leningrad in the early 1930s. It was based on the Great Tundra dialect spoken by the people living mostly in the Yamal-Nenets National (now Autonomous) Okrug. At first, Nenets books were published in roman type characters, then Cyrillic was introduced in 1939. Basic linguistic works which contributed to the establishment of standard Nenets are listed in the *Yurak Chrestomathy* by Professor Gyula Décsy (Décsy, 1966: 7), who conducts a graduate programme on Samoyed linguistics at the Department of Central Eurasian Studies of Indiana University, Bloomington.

Economy, society, world view

The Nenets people practise seasonal fishing and hunting, but it is reindeer breeding which is the foundation of their economy. The significance of reindeer in the life of the people is hard to overestimate: it provides food, clothing (leather and fur), shelter (skins to cover their movable homes) and transportation indispensable in tundra conditions. Reindeer images proliferate in Nenets folklore and crafts. According to scholars investigating the origin and age of the Nenets' reindeer economy, it was the Nenets who established and developed the unique material culture based on the reindeer economy, and who taught other people in the Arctic region their skills (Vasilevich and Levin, 1951; Vainshtein, 1986). No wonder the Nenets' material culture has been called the reindeer type of civilization (Kodolanyi, 1976).

As part of the reindeer economy, the people practised a nomadic way of life. In the past, the seasonal search for proper pastures forced them to move in spring towards the northern seashore, and in autumn towards the southern forests. Migration from one area to another and the choice of pastures were based on the people's empirical knowledge about a reasonable and productive utilization of the land's natural resources. Ie. Susoi, a native Nenets scholar, gave a detailed account of the traditional customs which secured the success of the economy and affected not only the lifestyle but also the moral and social values of the Nenets.

Nenets treat their tundra as a huge spacious home which they endeavour to save for future generations. They know every corner of their land and regard themselves as the guardians of the region's resources. Their hunting rules aim not at exterminating but rather saving animals. For example, they do not fire at certain birds and animals, trying instead to catch them while riding a sledge, so that only the weakest (those that would not survive anyway) become the hunter's victims. There are also restrictions on the quantity of animals which can be caught for fur, and on the areas where the hunting can take place. When a Nenets family leaves the nomad camp, they are careful to clean the area as they found it, perhaps with only a neat trace of fire (which they never start without any necessity). The Nenets have created many taboos for the purpose of protecting nature. To make the rules psychologically convincing they express them in the form of beliefs and superstitions. For example, the people believe that if these taboos are violated, thunderstorm, flood, rain or snow could start. The reindeer is a subject of many such taboos. Since good pasture is important for the herds, none of the Nenets picks so much as a blade of grass without a reason, although they are highly knowledgeable about the medicinal properties of plants and freely collect those that will be of use to them (Susoi, 1986: 113-22).

These unwritten laws and customs make the nomadic tribal life and economy efficient, and environmentally protective. They support the view of this culture as a positive and progressive phenomenon, a view which is often labelled by sceptics as romantic and idealistic.

The need to travel prompted the Nenets to create a mobile type of dwelling, suitable for their nomadic life. The conic tent called *choom* is constructed of a few poles, covered with reindeer skins in winter and birch bark in summer. The *choom* is usually a home for a family or sometimes a few related families. A camp of chooms, called *nesy*, comprises a group of travelling families related to each other and sharing the ownership of the reindeer herds.

The existence among the Samoyed of a social organization based on exogamous relationships was first pointed out in 1770s by Peter Pallas (Pallas, 1771-76). Subsequent studies described the exogamous rules and organization of clans into larger exogamous unities – phratries (Dolgikh, 1970b: 174). Marriage within one and the same clan and, moreover, the same phratry, was forbidden. Various terms were applied to the basic unit of the Nenets nomadic society: migratory band, clan, or tribe. Khomich accepts the term clan. She characterizes traditional Nenets society by exogamous patrilocal marriage, as well as patrimonial lineage, name, and ownership of pastures, sacrificial sites and cemeteries (Khomich, 1966: 142).

The world view of the Samoyed is based on a complex of animistic and totemistic beliefs, and a worship of spirits residing in the three worlds: the sky (the upper world), on the earth (the middle world), and under the ground (the underworld). The Samoyed express their philosophical outlook through various symbolic forms and behaviours – myths, song narratives, rites and ceremonies. As Galina Grachiova points out, learning the people's world view is similar to putting the many pieces of a puzzle together. It requires paying attention to all manifestations of the culture (Grachiova, 1984).

Although in the Nenets' mythological stories the image of the main creator of the world, the supernatural being *Num*, is often present, the religious ideology of the people conforms to the early form of religion, first described by Sir Edward Burnett Tylor, and later by Emil Durkheim (Tylor, 1871; Durkheim, 1915). The essence of this religion is the animation of nature and the belief that spirits reside in all aspects of nature. In the past, religious life was organized around a religious leader called a shaman, and his/her ritual activities. As in many other shamanistic traditions, Nenets shamans served as mediators between the people and the outside world. Their goals were to harmonize life within society, and conduct communication with nature and its spirits.

As a basis for analysis and explanation of the people's musical expression and behaviour, social and ideological aspects of the Nenets' traditional culture will be discussed in more detail in the following chapters.

Destruction of the Nenets' traditional society

In the 1990s, the Nenets, like other northern minorities of Russia, have found themselves in desperate conditions (Vakhtin, 1994: 31). The Russian ethnolinguist Nikolai Vakhtin has called for special attention to be paid to this situation. He points out that the history of the Nenets has been largely misrepresented in Soviet ethnographic studies, and he describes this misrepresentation as a gradual destruction of the traditional culture under the 'dark years' of the Soviet state. Although colonization of the aboriginal population began during tsarist Russia, it was the Soviet state which actually conquered the northern peoples, undermined their cultures, and left them with little hope for survival.

The expansion of tsarist Russia into North European regions was first recorded by chronicles of the 11th and 12th centuries, the time when the aboriginal people of the north paid taxes to the Novgorod state. Conflicts with the native population, among whom the Nenets were the most resilient and rebellious, accompanied Russian colonization. The process was completed at the beginning of the 17th century, when the territory populated by the Nenets was secured under the power of the Moscow state.

The Russian state was determined to control the indigenous Arctic peoples who often rebelled against the state and, particularly, the taxation (*yasak*) imposed on them. In a regulation on how to administer northern peoples, issued by the committee of Michael Speransky (the tsar's advisor) in 1822, the Nenets were assigned the status of *inorodets* (strangers). Although the rights of the people to self-regulation and land ownership are indicated in the document, they were never actually fulfilled.

In addition, an intrusion into the spiritual world of the Nenets was carried out through the missionary activities of the Orthodox Church. M. Castren and other scholars who visited the people in the early to mid nineteenth century announced the beginning of the 'extinction of the *inorodets* tribes of Siberia' (Castren, 1846; Iakoby, 1893; Khomich, 1966: 46). The situation grew worse when, in exchange for local goods, Russian dealers began supplying vodka in great quantities to the tundra. Alcoholism became a widespread problem, undermining many traditional cultural activities.

The collapse of tsarist Russia and the creation of the Soviet State brought further painful changes to the Nenets' way of life. Soon after its establishment, the Soviet government turned its attention to the task of governing and developing northern cultures, such as the Nenets. The Northern Committee was established in 1924 to deal with the task. It was initially decided by the Committee that recommendations by ethnographers, the experts on the northern and Siberian cultures, would be taken into consideration in the discussion of future reforms. Vladimir Bogoraz, who became a devoted researcher of the northern peoples and their cultures while living among them during his political exile (1890-98) as a member of an anti-tsarist organization 'The People's Will', proposed a plan for protecting the people's autonomy and their rights on the tundra land. He suggested the establishment of reservations to which access by migrating populations would be forbidden (Bogoraz-Tan, 1934). The Soviet government rejected this proposal, and soon after the Northern Committee was disbanded. The aboriginal cultures lost the opportunity of having an agency representing their interests in the Soviet government, which took full control of their land and resources. This set them on the way to the current crisis.

From the beginning of its establishment, the Soviet government proclaimed its intention to reform the life of the northern minorities. It justified these reforms by claiming that the traditional culture of the local peoples had no potential for future development. Underestimating the cultural achievements of the people, and completely ignoring the uniqueness of the existing cultural traditions, the government was reluctant to see an organic linkage and productive affinity between the ecology of these northern states and the traditional economic activities they practised.

The reforms initiated by the government proved to be the most serious attack yet on the fundamentals of the Nenets' existence: their nomadic way of life and shamanistic beliefs. The economy was reorganized in accordance with a 'kolkhoz'/'sovkhoz' system of maintaining stock-breeding and agriculture uniformly established all over the Soviet country. Disregarding the special geographical conditions of the social economy in the Arctic area, the government relocated the people, distributing them among primitively built settlements, and forcing them into a sedentary lifestyle, unsuitable for the way they handled their reindeer-breeding economy. In addition to these reforms, repressive action was taken against the shamans, who had provided a crucial role in maintaining the psychological well-being of the people and regulating their relationship with the environment.

The Nenets family unit, which had functioned to maintain cultural stability and continuity and to provide a stable educational environment for children, underwent a destructive transformation. Men travelling with herds had to live apart from their families for most of the year, while soon after birth children were placed in state boarding schools (*internats*). The transmission of cultural knowledge to the younger generation was disrupted and, as a result, there is now a lack of people with the skills essential for re-developing the reindeer economy once more.

Further damage to the culture and original ecology of the region was brought about by the arrival of industrial enterprises to the Arctic and Siberia. Contaminated rivers, pastures, and forests caused appalling ecological problems and left many people without traditional means of survival.

> 'Where shall we live, what shall we do, where shall we hunt and fish, where shall we get drinking water?' – these are the problems all northern minorities of Russia are currently facing to a lesser or greater extent (Vakhtin, 1994: 69).

The people's human rights were affected as well. Legally unprotected, they became exposed to assimilation and different kinds of discrimination by government officials (Vakhtin, 1994: 68).

Thus, during a relatively short period in the history of the Nenets' existence, the process of the destruction of the traditional culture complex has been almost completed. Enormous environmental, cultural, and demographic devastation characterize the state of all northern cultures of Russia after the collapse of the communist empire. In addition to the lost pastures, herds, and rivers, the people of North Eurasia suffer an accelerating decrease in population. There is a real threat to these individual nations' future existence if this trend proceeds any further.

Only after the democratization of Soviet society in the late 1980s did open discussions on the urgent problems of the northern nations become possible. Anxiety about the peoples' future was expressed in many articles published in the Russian press (Oborotova, 1988; Taksami, 1989; Sokolova, 1990a; 1990b). A group of ethnographers periodically raised alarm trying to attract attention to the plight of the people of North Eurasia, and proposing different programmes of action and reform which could save the nations and their original cultures. In such an atmosphere the Association of Northern Minorities was formed. Its first meeting took place in March 1990 in Moscow (Sokolova, 1990a: 142; Vakhtin, 1994: 72). Representatives of the Nenets nation made up the majority of the delegates present at the conference. As has always been the case throughout the history of Russian colonization of the Arctic, the Nenets lead other northern minorities in their political aspirations and spirit of independence.

State of research on the Nenets and their culture

Brief history of the research

The first ethnographic accounts of the Samoyed appear in the travelling notes, chronicles and annals of the 16th century.[3] In 1701, Semion Remezov, Russian geographer, ethnographer, and historian of Siberia, marked some of the Nenets' territories on his maps (Remezov, 1882). A series of research expeditions to Siberia conducted in the 18th century resulted in numerous descriptive accounts concerning the geography, geology, botany, ethnography and linguistics of the northern people. By the beginning of the 19th century, scholars had already gathered together much basic information on the Samoyed.

Archimandrite Benjamin, the chief of the Orthodox mission in 1825, was responsible for converting the Nenets of the Kanin, Malaia Zemlia, and Bol'shaia Zemlia tundras of Archangel province to Christianity. While trying to change the people's religious beliefs and activities, he was at the same time interested in studying the Nenets' language and religion. Following his linguistic research among Mezen' Samoyeds, he translated the scriptures into Nenets. His manuscript grammar of Nenets became an important source of information for many future researchers (Benjamin, 1858).

A major contribution to the studies on the Samoyed was made by the Finno-Ugrian scholar Matthias Castren (1813-52). Castren's interest in the past history of the Finno-Ugrian peoples led him to expand his research into the area of Samoyed linguistics. During the expeditions of 1842-43 and 1845-49, organized by the Russian Academy of Science, he collected a significant amount of data on the language and ethnography of the Yurak-Nenets.

The establishment of the Siberian division of the Russian Geographical Society in 1845 intensified the research on the Samoyed. Ethnographers under the auspices of this society, as well as some foreign travellers, provided an ethnographic description of different groups of the Nenets (Islavin, 1847; Czaplicka, 1914).

During the Soviet period the northern cultures were, for the most part, only accessible to Soviet scholars, who made significant progress in linguistic and ethnographic research in this area. A unique contribution to the field of study was made by Grigory Verbov, who was destined to die in battle during the Second World War. Verbov collected original data on the exogamy and kinship relationships among the Nenets, and described the least-known group, the Forest Nenets, thus providing an invaluable information for various future studies on Samoyed cultures (Verbov, 1936; 1939; 1973). The first scholarly grammars of the Nenets, the Enets, the Sel'kup, and the Nganasan were compiled by Georgy Prokof'iev.

All studies on the history and culture of the Samoyed published after the Second World War were framed within Marxist-Leninist ideology. Despite this biased approach, these studies contain significant and indispensable ethnographic information still valid today. Among these publications were the volume *Narody Sibiri* [The Peoples of Siberia] edited by Maksim Levin and Leoind Potapov, later translated into English (1956; 1964); *Ocherki Etnicheskoi Istorii Pechorskogo Kraia* [Essays on the Ethnic History of the Pechora Region] by Lev Lashook (1958); and a series of articles and monographs on the origin and social organization of the Samoyed by Dolgikh (1952; 1960; 1962; 1970a; 1970b). The 1966 monograph *Nentsy* [The Nenets] by Khomich offered a comprehensive survey of the state of research on the Nenets' culture and society. However, it presented a history of the Nenets consistent with that promoted by the government, which declared that the Soviet state had liberated the people from their backward past and had provided them with a better standard of living and the chance of a prosperous future.

Western scholars concentrated on exploring the historical relationship between the Finno-Ugrian and Samoyed peoples. Comparing the peoples' customs, linguistic structures and etymologies, they aimed at discovering the ethnic origin of the peoples (Bouda, 1940; Angere, 1956; Hajdu, 1962).

The problem of ethnic origin

The problem of determining the ethnic origins of the Samoyed was an important issue for Finno-Ugrian, Russian, and Soviet researchers. Theories began to flourish towards the end of the 18th century, when the members of the expedition to Siberia and Kamchatka (1768-74) discovered people speaking Samoyed languages (Koibal, Soiot, Motor, Tubin, Kamachin, Karakass) on the northern side of the Sayan mountains (Miller, 1937). By the middle of the 19th century, these languages had been ousted by Turkic languages and began to disappear altogether. However, researchers continued to be fascinated by their original existence, and this fascination promted a variety of different and sometimes contradictory theories. In 1730, Philipp Strahlenberg suggested that the Samoyed peoples were originally aboriginal inhabitants of the north and that they had later moved to the south (Strahlenberg, 1730).

An opposing view was proposed by Iohann Fisher in 1774, who suggested that the ancestors of the North Eurasian Samoyed were Samoyed tribes who had inhabited the Sayan plateau and who had eventually moved to the north (Fisher, 1774). Over 70 years later, this idea was revived by Castren based on additional supporting evidence (Castren, 1856).

The Fisher-Castren theory, however, did not take into account the role played by the aboriginal pre-Samoyed population of the northern tundra and taiga in the origin of the Samoyed. This oversight was corrected after the archeological excavations on the Yamal peninsula conducted by Valery Chernetsov in 1929 (Chernetsov, 1935), when some traces of an aboriginal northern culture *sirtia* were discovered. As the name *sirtia* is often encountered in the Nenets' folklore, it was assumed that the *sirtia* were the aboriginal people assimilated by the southern Samoyed tribes. Elaborating on the discoveries, Prokof'iev suggested that when the southern Samoyed moved to the north they met and eventually intermixed with some aboriginal people which determined the division of the Samoyed into the Nenets, the Enets, the Sel'kup, and the Nganasan. This theory found support in the works of many other scholars (Briusov, 1952; Foss, 1952; Dolgikh, 1952; Lashook, 1958; 1968; Vasil'iev, 1970).

Opponents of the Fisher-Castren theory who did not believe in the southern origin of the Samoyed adhered to the idea, first proposed by Strahlenberg, that Siberia was not the original, but the eventual homeland of the Samoyed, who most likely migrated in the opposite direction, from the north to the south (Bubrikh, 1948; Hajdu, 1953; Okladnikov, 1957; Dul'zon, 1961).

Khomich supported the Sayan origin of the northern Samoyed. In her account of Nenets history, the Nenets' ancestors left the Sayan mountains in the first millennium AD, some time during a large migration of various peoples in this geographical area. They came to the northern seashore along the Ob' River, most likely in the second part of the first millenium. Here they encountered the aboriginals (*sirtia*) mentioned in the Nenets' legends. The first wave of the newcomers developed into the Enets and the Nganasan, the second wave formed the foundation of the Nenets, and the last became the Sel'kup. While establishing themselves in the north as a nation, these peoples developed a common foundation for all aspects of their tundra culture: their reindeer economy, their language, their religious beliefs and their cults, marriage customs and kinship structure (Khomich, 1966: 35-41).

Folklore research

Research on Nenets folklore has always been closely bound up with research into the ethnic origin of the Samoyed in general. Since folklore proved to be an indispensable source of information for ethnographers, historians, linguists, and other experts, an increasing number of scholars with different skills and expertise became involved in the task of collecting and studying Nenets folklore.

Castren was the first to pay attention to Nenets folklore. During his expeditions of 1842-43 and 1845-49, he collected samples of Nenets folklore which were published posthumously by Toivo Lehtisalo (Lehtisalo, 1940; 1960). In the first part of the book, twelve Nenets texts, mostly in epic genre, were presented. The second part contained eight Sel'kup texts. As a result of his own trip to the Tundra and Forest Nenets in 1911-12 and 1914, Lehtisalo published a collection of 285 Nenets folklore texts, including sacrificial prayers, and shamanic songs and tales which are rarely performed today (Lehtisalo, 1947).

Extensive studies on Nenets folklore were conducted during the 1930s by Prokof'iev, Professor of the Leningrad State University, and his students Pyrerka, Verbov, Tereshchenko, and Savel'iev. The work of this team was interrupted by the Second World War, during which much of the research materials they had collected disappeared: Prokof'iev died in the siege of Leningrad; Pyrerka, Verbov, and Savel'iev were killed in combat. Some of their research, however, survives in the Archives of the Institute of Ethnography of the Russian Academy of Science in St Petersburg.

Research work on Nenets folklore was resumed as soon as the war was over. In 1946, under the auspices of the Soviet Geographical Society and the supervision of Shcherbakova, an expedition to Malaia Zemlia and Bol'shaia Zemlia was organized. Only a part of the materials collected in this trip was published later by Kupriianova, a philologist and a folklorist, the author of the first monograph on Nenets epic poetry (1965: 15, fn.). Among other scholars continuing the work, the most productive authors were Tereshchenko, an expert on Samoyed languages and the wife of Pyrerka, Khomich, and Kupriianova. During 1960s and 1970s, Nenets students (Bobrikova, Latysheva, Ledkov, Pichkov, Susoi, Pushkariova, and others) became actively involved in folklore research. As a result of this collective effort, a lot of collected material was preserved and stored in the local Houses of Folklore located within the Nenets National Okrug.

After the development of the modern standard literary form of the Nenets language by Prokof'iev in the 1930s (Décsy, 1966), a number of collections of Nenets song texts, riddles, tales, and legends were published and adapted for educational purposes (Tonkov, 1936; Verbov, 1937; Tereshchenko, 1949; 1954; Shcherbakova, 1960). The first scholarly publication concerning Nenets folklore was undertaken by Kupriianova, who presented her research on Nenets epic songs in a monograph which she published with herself in 1965. In the book's introduction, the author provided both her own and the Nenets people's classification of the folklore genres. Kupriianova analysed the content, function and form of the oral performances of the songs and found ten genre categories: epic narratives, sacrificial prayers and charms, legends, ritual poetry, shamanic songs and tales, magic tales, epic songs, lyrical songs, riddles, and modern narratives (1965: 19). As for the native approach to classification, Kupriianova emphasized that Nenets performers were very consistent in using their terminology, which clearly differentiated between musical or non-musical forms of performance. For example: spoken prose narratives are called *vadako*, or *lachanako*, whereas for the sung genres, there exists a special terminology: *iangebts* is song, in general; *khynnabts* is the Nenets' song in general; *iarabts* is a lament; *siudbabts* is a song about giants; *sio* means just a voice, and as such it is used with adjectives or possessives, for example, children's *sio*, drunk *sio* (1965: 21). Kupriianova then focuses on two categories of epic song, *siudbabts* and *iarabts*, and lyrical song improvisations, *khynnabts*, which are more flexible in content and performed on any occasion. She also describes the typical plots and characters, compositional technique, and formulaic expressions in the texts of the epic songs, and outlines the historical development of Nenets epics from the archaic *siudbabts* to the later *iarabts*. Kupriianova's conclusion is that the Nenets' epic song tradition is becoming extinct.

> In our days the Nenets epic remains the art of the past age, and the young generation will learn it from books (Kupriianova, 1965: 56).

The most recent philological study of the Nenets' epics is a posthumous publication of some of the song texts compiled by Tereshchenko in 1990. Introducing epic songs recorded in the western parts of the tundra, this book provides more accurate transcriptions of the poetic form of the song performances (Tereshchenko, 1990).

Musicological research on songs

Musical research began as a collection and preservation activity pursued by various ethnospecialists who made a large number of recordings of Nenets songs, which are now housed in archives in Finland and Russia.[4] The majority of these recordings have not yet been subjected to a thorough analysis.

As a first step, musicologists began to transcribe and publish the recordings made by other fieldworkers. The first significant product of this work was a scholarly publication of Nenets melodies by the Finnish ethnomusicologist Armas Väisänen who transcribed the phonograms made by the two Finno-Ugrian linguists, Lehtisalo (1887-1962) and Donner (1888-1935) during their expeditions to Siberia in 1911-14. The fifty-six melodic transcriptions were given in this publication without their texts, since, as Väisänen explained in his introduction, the words in the original recordings were not clearly pronounced. Väisänen could not indicate where these songs were recorded or who had performed them, because the collectors' notes lacked this information (Väisänen, 1965: vi). In this collection of musical transcriptions, Väisänen implemented the same methods of transcription which he used previously in his other transcribed collection of songs, *Mordwinische Melodien* [Mordvinian Melodies] of 1948. To enable clearer comparison of the songs, he transposed all the melodies into the same major and minor keys (G and E). Metre signification was applied only to those melodies which did show rhythmical regularities, otherwise the author considered the notation feature inappropriate.

At almost the same time, a similar work was completed by the Soviet folklorist Boris Dobrovol'sky, who compiled a musical supplement to Kupriianova's monograph (Dobrovol'sky, 1965: 757-80). Dobrovol'sky transcribed six epic song melodies and annotated his transcriptions. He described the musical style of each of the selected songs, discussed the relation of the melodies to the texts, and attempted to classify the melodies into types. The author put the melodies into keys identical with the tonal levels of the performances (yet he transposed the melodies one octave higher to avoid textual inconveniences), and used a combination of metre signatures to indicate metrical irregularities.

A separate place belongs to publications made as a result of various authors' field trips to the Nenets tundra. To the best of my knowledge, Soviet professional musicians first went to the Nenets tundra in 1938. Two Soviet composers, Grigory Frid and Isaak Shteinman, visited the Yamal peninsula where they recorded a few Nenets songs on phonograph cylinders. The recordings are now in the possession of the Cabinet of Folk Music in the Moscow Conservatory. In an article written in as late as 1990, Frid characterizes the Nenets' musical tradition as primitive and hardly worthy of interest, justifying his view by a lack of polyphony or any other sophisticated structural features which, in his opinion, are the only indications of a high level of musical creativity (Frid, 1991).

In 1970s, the Soviet composer and folklorist Igor' Bogdanov became active in collecting the musical folklore of the northern people of Russia in general, and the Nenets in particular. Protected by copyright law, his recordings are stored in the Phonogram Archives of the Union of the Soviet Composers in Moscow. Bogdanov reflected on the Nenets music he collected in a couple of articles (Bogdanov, 1978; 1982).

A few more articles on the musical style of the Nenets' song tradition came out as a result of my trips to the European Nenets in 1975-76 (Gomon, 1980; 1990; 1992). The same musical data is now subjected to a more comprehensive analysis.

Among all the articles dedicated to Nenets song, the one by N. Vakhitova stands out as the first publication of the songs of the Forest Nenets (Vakhitova, 1989). Seven rare songs performed by two native performers, themselves scholars, were recorded and analysed by the author with special attention paid to the melodies' 'segmentation' and 'syntax'. A later account of the Nenets' music in Russian appeared in a brief survey of the musical cultures of the northern peoples by Yu. Sheikin (Sheikin, 1996: 23-5).[5]

A summary of all the published materials mentioned above and a survey of musical recordings available in the Archives of Finland and Russia were provided in a master's thesis by Jarkko Niemi, a student of the Department of Folk Tradition of the University of Tampere, Finland (Niemi, 1992). The thesis, written in Finnish, became the first overview of the state of research on Nenets musical culture. An extended version of this study was published in 1998 as a doctoral dissertation (Niemi, 1998).

Scholars from fields adjacent to ethnomusicology addressed the musical aspects of the songs as well. Two essays, 'The Nenets Shaman Song and its Text' by Hajdu (1978) and 'Shaman Songs and Worldview' by Grachiova (1984), deserve special acknowledgement as the most provocative studies on Nenets' song, which succeed in blurring the boundaries between different disciplines. Hajdu reveals a unique feature of the melody/word relationship in the Nenets songs, whereas Grachiova introduces the attitudes and the concepts about music held among the Samoyed, so shedding light on the function and value of musical expression in this culture.

Research on Musical Instruments

The above survey shows that song has been the main concern of all specialists interested in the Nenets' musical culture. However, the fact that no attempt has been made by scholars to explore the world of Nenets musical instruments can be explained. By the time musicologists started to pay attention to this musical culture, no signs of instrumental performance practice among the Nenets were left available for observation. The instruments which had previously existed had all passed out of use, along with the religious practices to which they had been intimately attached. The only source of information on this subject available today are the writings of ethnographers, published at various times, which describe and analyse shamanic paraphernalia and, of course, those musical instruments collected by ethnographers and now preserved in museums.

Although there was available evidence (Dioszegi, 1978: 144-5) of the existence of such instruments as the jaw harp and musical bow among the people of the Sayan mountains (the homeland of the Samoyed tribes in the distant past), the only cult instrument observed among the North Samoyed peoples was a framed type of drum (or tambourine), together with a stick.

A large number of articles on shamanic drums pointed to the clear similarities between the different versions of this instrument among the Samoyed and other North Eurasian and Siberian peoples; this comparison enabled scholars to make a reasonably accurate reconstruction of the drum used by the Nenets. The drum consisted of a wooden frame bent into a round, oval or elliptical form, and a drumstick. It was a crucial symbol of shamanism decorated with drawings that provided a glimpse into the mythology and cosmology of the vanished culture. The drum itself was identified with a reindeer, horse, or boat, while the drumstick was a symbol for a whip or an oar.

Hundreds of shamanic drums among the Lapps, Nenets and other northern nations were burnt at different times by Christian missionaries and Soviet officials, but approximately 75 drums were preserved in museums across the world. Ernst Emsheimer considered the shamanic drum a very important source of ethnographic information about the Arctic peoples. Whilst he admitted that knowledge about the musical performances of the past involving the sound of the drum is limited, he nevertheless formulated theories about the symbolic role of the instrument among the Lapps and

Khakass, based on 'what is known about the North Eurasian drum in general' (Emsheimer, 1964; 1991a; 1991c).

Some ethnographers, however, did hear the sound of the drum in its natural setting. Donner, for example, on his trips to Siberian Samoyeds at the beginning of this century (1911-14), had an opportunity to listen to 'the dull roar of the magic drum' and watched an 'expert handling of the drum' by shamans (Donner, 1954: 68). But most of the ethnographic research on the drum, especially that done after the 1930s, simply consists of analyses of museum objects. These studies treat the drawings and the names of the drums as a source for various reconstructions (Dioszegi, 1968; 1978; Potapov, 1970; 1978; Joki, 1978; Dolgikh, 1978; Basilov, 1984). The most comprehensive account of the use of the drum in shamanistic traditions was given by Iekaterna Prokof'ieva, who described, analysed, and classified the structure of the instrument into types (Prokof'ieva, 1961). The author gave attention to every ethnic type of the drum, including that of the Nenets. In her description, the Nenets' version of the drum (called *penzer*, *pender*, *tadiber-penzer*) has a round (rarely oval) shape, is of a small size (50-60 cm in diameter), with a frame made of larch or fir, covered with the skin of a wild reindeer, and with a handle inside rather than outside the drum. The author reveals the symbolic features of the drum. Made of a 'branch' of a reindeer horn, the handle inside the drum divides the round space of the instrument into the three areas representing the shamanic cosmological model of the universe, consisting of the upper-, middle- and under-worlds (Prokof'ieva, 1961: 437).

Today, we can find Nenets singers-narrators describing scenes in which the shaman's drum plays its sacred role.

> 'The woman with the light head,
> Bring me my shamanic drum from the sacred *narta*!'
> The drum is brought.
> As it is dropped on the metal cross-beams of the *choom*,
> The giant drum begins singing by itself.
> I take the drum with my two hands, and say:
> 'The woman with the light head, follow me.'
> The words of my vows are flowing like a river.
> Those outside who hear the sound enter the *choom*.
> While singing I leave nothing unsolved
> On the earth and in the sky (Tereshchenko, 1990: 54).

Yet this sacred shamanic instrument has already become a thing of the past. Its absence from the Nenets' musical culture today raises an intriguing question as to how different the songs that have survived are to those which would have been accompanied by the magic drum in the past.

Any discussion of such differences was hypothetical before new evidence was reported by A. Saifutdinova. In 1995, she was fortunate to record two *khynnabts* songs by F. Ardeiev, Nar'ian Mar, who accompanied himself on the drum (Saifutdinova, 1998: 60-61).[6] In her article, Saifutdinova described two different types of melody/drum correlation. One of the recorded performances featured drum accompaniment synchronically duplicating the rhythm of vocal melody. Another performance was characterized by a persistent discrepancy between the rhythms of the vocal part and its drum accompaniment. The evidence found by Saifutdinova did not prevent her from emphasizing the overwhelmingly vocal character of the Nenets' music.

Notes

1. Nenets epic song 'Eight Jarko' (Tereshchenko, 1990: 54).
2. The Nenets and their culture have been described in a number of general and special volumes (Prokof'ieva, 1956: 608-47; 1964: 547-70; Hajdu, 1963; Khomich, 1966). The *Human Relation Area Files* include concise ethnographic data on the Yurak-(Nenets)-Samoyed first introduced by G. Murdock in his *Ethnographic Atlas* (1967: 86-7). Updated demographic and ethnographic information on the Nenets can be obtained from the two recently published books on the polar peoples and Arctic adaptation (Vakhtin, 1994: 29-80; Krupnik, 1989; 1993).
3. Referring to Hackluyt's Collection, vol.1, London, 1809: 274, Khomich mentions that in 1556 Captain Steven Burrough took a trip to the river Ob'. On the island of Vaigach he discovered about 300 religious idols which belonged to a Samoyed people (Khomich, 1964: 6).
4. Among the archives are the Phonogram Archives of the Institute of Russian Literature (Pushkin House) in St Petersburg; the Cabinet of Folk Music in the Moscow Conservatory; the Archives of the Union of the Soviet Composers; the Archives of Radio centres and the local Houses of Folklore in the administrative towns of the Nenets tundra.
5. Reference to the book was provided by Izaly I. Zemtsovsky.
6. Reference to the article was provided by Izaly I. Zemtsovsky.

CHAPTER TWO

Performance Practice

Dear mother!
I've been moaning and moaning:
They brought us to this settlement forever,
I may never again ride my four-reindeer narta![1]

Song in the life of the people

To observe the Nenets song tradition in practice, I visited two Nenets settlements located in the European part of the Arctic tundra – Nel'min Nos and Indiga. To reach these remote places, I had to fly first to Nar'ian Mar, the only town in the tundra that had an airport,[2] and then take a helicopter to my final destinations.

The town of Nar'ian Mar was founded in 1929. Its name, meaning 'Red Town', was given by Lenin, who promised an improved way of life for the Nenets people. Replacing a former village, Nar'ian Mar marked the unification of the European Nenets of Malaia Zemlia and Kanin-Timan tundras into the Nenets Autonomous National District.

When I arrived in Nar'ian Mar in March 1975, I saw a small, snow-covered wooden town. It was populated mostly by Russians who were engaged in governmental services, small industries, cultural and educational organizations, and communication media. Bilingual Nenets accounted for the smallest percentage of the population; many of them were involved in traditional crafts turned into commercial enterprises.

The life of the entire tundra reverberated in this small town. Wherever you went you heard the news coming in from all the different tundra settlements. Nar'ian Mar appeared to be extremely busy, coordinating the life of this vast frozen land filled with working people constantly on the move. However, to get access to the settlements was not easy, especially during winter time. The only way of transportation was by air, and flights were, like every other activity in the tundra, subject to weather conditions.

It was at Nar'ian Mar airport that I met a colourful crowd of people dressed in ethnic costumes, including *malitsa* (fur coat) and *pimy* (fur shoes) made of reindeer skins. Some of the dresses looked casual, others were beautifully trimmed with fur mosaic and ornaments. I later discovered that these people were some of the finest exponents of Nenets song. After visiting Nar'ian Mar for one reason or another, they were anxious to get back home. Sometimes, the whole family made the trip together: there were grandparents, parents with young children, and pets in the helicopter taking us to Nel'min Nos, the settlement closest to Nar'ian Mar.

Nel'min Nos

Nel'min Nos (literally, Nel'min's nose) is situated on the banks of the Pechora River. According to a local legend, when the people first came to the place, they threw a net into the river. Only one fish, Nel'ma, was pulled out, but even that single one swam away. The people were left in the lurch, or, in the equivalent Russian idiom, 'left with a nose', here meaning left with the Nel'ma-fish's nose.

In 1929, the settlement became the first to have a Soviet deer-breeding *kolkhoz* [collective farm]. Later this *kolkhoz* was named after one of its founders, the Nenets man I. P. Vyucheisky, who was murdered in 1936 (Khomich, 1966: 236).

Famous for its still extant epic tradition, Nel'min Nos had played host to numerous ethnographers and folklorists for a number of years. Kupriianova, prior to publishing her volume of Nenets epic texts, visited the place three times. It was not, therefore, surprising that the town's people showed a full understanding of my work there, and made frequent offers of help.

First of all, they transformed a room in the kolkhoz office into a boarding room for me. The door of the office was never closed, and even during the night people would come into the office to use the only phone in the settlement. Despite such inconveniences, the place was an excellent location for observing the daily and nightly life of the community: how business problems were solved, or how treatment for the sick was provided. Soon after the news of my arrival had spread around, Natalia Taleieva, at that time in her 40s, a representative of a famous dynasty of epic singers, came to the office with her friends and offered to sing for me.

Responding to my questions about other local performers, people directed me to the homes of Andrei Vyucheisky, Maria Iavtysaia, and Timofei Sobolev. Winter seemed to provide perfect conditions for the song recordings, as it made all these people sit at their homes most of the time. Sometimes, however, severe weather conditions created a shortage of electricity that hampered work with my reel-to-reel tape recorder, which did not run on batteries.

By the time I had used all my tape cassettes and was ready to leave the town, the weather had become worse, and helicopters stopped arriving at the settlement. After a few days waiting for the weather to improve, I happened to look out of the window of my room and saw a helicopter landing on a snow valley half a mile away. The helicopter was delivering mail to the tundra by throwing it on snow-fields. It was quite unusual for it to make a landing. I flung my belongings into a case and started running towards the helicopter through the waist-deep snow, while waving my hands and trying to attract the pilot's attention. The propellers were already spinning when I reached the helicopter. In a minute I was flying away from the people who had so generously favoured me with their invaluable songs.

This first, rather experimental, trip to the tundra taught me how tough living conditions in Nenets settlements were, and I resolved to come better equipped on my next visit.

Indiga

While looking at the map of the Nenets National District, I was intrigued by a tiny dot named *Indiga* at the very edge of the mainland, the most northern point of the Kanin Peninsula. The settlement was built on the banks of the river which carried the same name (see plate 1 and 4). An alternative native toponym, *pe jaxa harad* (a home on a stone river) referred to the people's sense of belonging to the river.

I arrived at Indiga a year after the trip to Nel'min Nos. Luckily, the weather was unusually bright for the tundra and everything was shining under the polar sun: the white plateau, the river with its high, steep banks joined by a rope-bridge, and the settlement nestled on a distant hill across the river. The northern scenery was majestic. But it did not take long to discover the other side to this wild beauty.

To reach the settlement I had to pass across the rope bridge which hangs high above the icy surface of the river, swaying with the wind. I later learned that the only well providing drinking water for Indiga was located on the opposite side of the river to the settlement, making even the collection of this simple necessity a hazardous task.

The Russians running the administrative and cultural life of the *sovkhoz* [Soviet farm] in Indiga were surprisingly young. A man who introduced himself as the chairman of the *sovkhoz* looked like a teenager, as did a young teacher of the elementary school, Ludmila, who offered me shelter in her home. The local people took an interest in my work, but, unlike the residents of Nel'min Nos, they could not recollect anybody who had ever come to Indiga to study their native songs.

My stay in Indiga was extremely rewarding. Unlike my experience in Nel'min Nos, when the people had been locked inside their homes because of the blizzard, the weather this time allowed the people of Indiga to spend time outside. I was, therefore, able to observe more aspects of village life: I watched one of my singers constructing a boat in his yard and a group of women sitting on the steps of a house, enjoying the sun and decorating their *malitsas* with glass beads.

The singers I worked with, Fiodor Belugin and Iekaterina Belugina, Semion Apitsin, Maria Argeieva, and Ulita Apitsina, were skilful masters of musical performance. Their song repertories seemed inexhaustible, while their ability to instantaneously improvise was a sign of their artistic ingenuity. Almost everybody had a unique manner of singing, but dignity, modesty, and inspiration characterized all of them. When the blind singer Semion Apitsin was approaching the exciting peaks in his performances, I could not resist naming him the Nenets' Homer. The song improvisation which I recorded in Indiga were long and thought-provoking.

My hostess, Ludmila, told me that she enjoyed life in Indiga and that she would not even consider living anywhere else. Most of the people in that place felt the same way. Despite the severe life conditions, they developed a deep attachment to the northern land.

Song and poverty

During my trips to the Nenets tundra, I became increasingly aware of a bitter irony. There was a striking contrast between the kinds of riches the Nenets people could offer to the outside world, and the low standard of living they experienced.

The Nenets produced many products which were expensive on the world market. In addition to deer-breeding, they had developed profitable industries, such as fur-farming, fishing, and sea-hunting. Moreover, they lived on a land rich in natural resources. Geologists had already begun mining the tundra for gold and coal, and the growth in the number of mines became one of the reasons why the Soviet government declared the zone closed. One could not even visit Nar'ian Mar without special permission from the local KGB office. Obediently, the Nenets were giving away the wealth they owned and produced. But what did they get in return?

The people lived in terrible poverty. Their homes lacked any elementary modern household technology, and their food stores were empty. The notable exception was vodka which always seemed to be available. Private hunting and fishing were officially prohibited, so in order to avoid starvation the Nenets pursued their traditional way of obtaining nutrition. I often saw families at their dinner tables, eating and drinking raw reindeer flesh and blood, which contained all the vitamins indispensable for the people's survival in the severe climate. There were other remnants of the old life-style. In many homes the Nenets were still sleeping on and under reindeer skins, as they did while living in *chooms*.

Clearly, the Soviet reforms had not delivered the material advantages they had promised. The Soviet state had proved adept in maximizing the use of local labor and land resources, with little or no benefit to the people themselves who were forced to participate in the erosion of their own traditional way of life, with any profit going to line the pockets of the Soviet government.

Song was the only wealth which was not taken away from the Nenets people. Soviet officials were, for the most part, too preoccupied with problems arising from religious discontent to take much notice of the Nenets' musical culture and the connection between the shamanistic religion and traditional song. Although the shamans were annihilated, the songs were left alone. The bilingual Nenets never became bimusical, and their songs survived intact and unique.

Herbert Tampere, the renowned researcher of Estonian song, once made an observation that it was typical for people experiencing a lot of hardship to have a sensitive character and inclination to express their feelings in song. In this statement, he generalized his experience of finding excellent song performers mostly among poor Estonian peasants, rather than among rich people in the villages (Tampere, 1983: 14). Both sensitivity and hardship are characteristic of Nenets singers as well. Indeed, they characterize the Nenets as a nation. Everyone in the Nenets tundra sings, although the degree of inspiration and sensitivity among the singers varies. Those who sing like real artists attract audiences, others just sing for themselves on a more regular basis.

All Nenets performers adhere to an elaborate and consistent terminology related to the songs, which testifies to the importance of song in the life of the people. The differentiation between the songs depends on the type of performing situation. Song-improvisations which men and women of different ages perform regularly on an everyday basis are called *sio* or *khynnabts*. The impulses to perform one of these songs are varied: whatever a person is seeing, watching, feeling or contemplating may stimulate such song improvisation.

As the Nenets often spend time in solitude, it is natural for them to sing to themselves, when they are alone at home, moving on their sledges through the tundra, or pasturing reindeer. This intimate song performance has an enormous therapeutic effect on the people who must endure the endless light or darkness of the polar nights and days. In such extreme conditions, songs spring from a person spontaneously, without the need for an audience.[3]

Epic songs hold a special status among the Nenets. They are taken very seriously by those who perform and those who listen. No matter how fantastic the narrated events may be, they are perceived as a real truth, something which indeed happened in the past. These performances fall into the pattern of bard/audience relationship, regularly encountered in musical cultures across the world. All of the audience's attention is concentrated on a singer creating a narrative. Although the audience emotionally reflects on the narrated events, stimulating and encouraging the performer by its reaction, its main function is to 'consume' the outcome, rather than participating in the creation of the song. The role of the bard is superior to the audience in this situation. The bard is a leader of the ritual of musical performance, but as in a West European concert, just listening – co-experiencing and taking the content to heart – has a value in itself.

The Nenets love their epic performances, which may break out anywhere, mostly at leisure time during fall and winter. I saw tears in the eyes of Fiodor Belugin's wife, listening to her husband singing an epic story. She was quietly sitting in the corner of the room when I began recording the performance. Gradually she became absorbed in the content of the song, expressing her involvement with gestures and sighs of relief.

In the home of Iekaterina Belugina, I caught the whole family at a dinner table. Everybody stayed after dinner to listen to her songs. Even her grandchildren became unusually quiet, afraid of disturbing the singer. The shared excitement of the performer and listeners was not surprising: the family had a chance to hear an outstanding female singer who could compete with the best performers of the national epics (see Plates 3 and 6).

Semion Apitsin had an appearance of a blind beggar: his clothing and his home could not create a more striking image of poverty, social neglect and abuse (see Plate 2). Compared to Apitsin, Fiodor Belugin, dressed in a beautiful malitsa, looked like a nobleman (see Plate 5). He was always full of energy and proud of whatever he was doing. The people in the settlement had great respect for both men, well known as the best singers in the community. Yet Apitsin was rated highest. His magic transformations from a poor and often drunk man into a powerful bard were impressive. Obviously, the people's respect for the singers was not determined by any socio-economic factor. They were all in the same boat – suppressed by the Soviet state but secured by their traditional beliefs and values. No wonder that the talents glorifying the traditions of the previous generations were granted an exclusive status in their communities.

Family ties are still very strong among the Nenets. Usually, the light of the performers' success and mastery falls on the image and memory of their family. More than once I heard people comparing a song they had just heard with a similar one sung in the past by a relative from the same family tradition.

In this respect, it is important to point out that the names of almost all the performers I recorded have an association with some of the names carried by the former Nenets clans. According to the list compiled by Verbov, there are eighteen such clan names (Dolgikh, 1970a: 10-11). While it is certainly easy to associate Maria Iavtysaia with the clan *Tysyia*, Andrei Vyucheisky with the clan *Vyutsi*, and Nataliia Taleieva with the clan *Talei*, other names require a special analysis of the clan relationship and may not sound similar to the original name. For example, according to Dolgikh's analysis, the people holding the name Apitsin belong to the clan *Vera*.

When I visited the Nenets tundra, a special status was still assigned to the people inheriting the shamanic profession, which often remained within a family. The punishment of shamans by the state had not yet faded in the people's memories, and, as a result, the people resisted talking about everything related to shamanism. Nevertheless, Tikhon Apitsin once told me a story about his painful beginning as a song performer. He recalled his suffering and hiding from his family during his adolescence. Once, while being alone in the tundra, he first sang a song to release the tension. This confession of Apitsin recalls many existing descriptions of the initial suffering and calling of shamans.[4] It indicates that the Nenets' shamanistic tradition is not completely abolished. It lives on in the form of the artistic expression of its talented devotees.

My acquaintance with Nenets song in its original setting helped me better realize the existing conditions of the song tradition, the unfairness, indeed irrelevance, of the attitudes towards it. These attitudes ranged from a complete neglect by educated philistines sceptical about any musical value of the folk song tradition to a scholarly curiosity of ethnographers and folklorists who studied mostly the verbal aspect of the songs. They rarely discussed the musicality of the people as a phenomenon of any value in understanding the people's mentality and culture.

The roads which could let Nenets melodies reach the outside world were not paved, and the musical sounds had no chance to cross the borders of the Nenets' homeland. While there were many young Nenets who became professionals in various fields, there was not one, to the best of my knowledge, who pursued the career of a professional musician. Not a single Nenets was enrolled in the four-year Music College in Archangel, the closest musical educational institution to the Nenets National District. Hardly popular among the Soviet composers, Nenets song had no opportunity to be incorporated into art music in the way that other folk traditions inspired professional composers.

On the other hand, as a result of the people's poverty, Nenets song was quite safe from the influence of other musical styles. Since the Nenets never had a chance to enjoy any modern means of communication with the outside world (I never saw a TV set or tape-recorder in Nenets homes), the process of change affecting musical cultures all around the world never reached the Nenets tundra. The people kept re-experiencing their traditional world in the musical style of previous generations. The destruction of the Nenets' religious and ritual life had limited the song performances to secular settings only, but the traditional techniques of music making had survived without any damage. The Nenets' singers still maintained a high artistic quality of performance, and from the point of view of quality, they were keeping their 'little' tradition great.[5] Song on its part helped the people survive the tragic occupation of their land and the devastating attack on their culture and spirituality.

The private rite of musical expression

A number of theories in ethnomusicology, folklore, and cultural anthropology highlight the emergent quality of performance, the role of extra-musical behaviour of participants, both performer and audience, and the significance of concrete performance situations, all highly revealing of culture and meaningful beyond the textual content of the performances (Merriam, 1964; Abrahams, 1975; Bauman, 1975; Behague, 1984; Bruner, 1986). The theories postulate that the study of music based on methods of observation and participation in the performance event enhances our knowledge of music as a manifestation of culture, and sheds light on the variety of cultural patterns of musical behaviour and communication. Within this tradition of thought, much emphasis has been placed on the experiential aspect of performance and the emergence of meaning in the present rather than in the past (Bruner, 1986: 3-30). Any performed expression unavoidably establishes some connections and bridges with current reality, and by observation musical ethnographers are able to determine and ultimately explain the emerging correlation between cultural reality, experience, and resultant expression. Meaning is 'always in the present, in the here-and-now'. There are 'no limits on meaning' in a performance situation, in which participants break through the everyday routine into the extraordinary and the more intense (Bruner, 1986: 11, 24).

However, the benefits of these theories postulating the primary role of fieldwork and musical ethnography do not eliminate a difficulty of interpretation of the field data. There is no theory meant to provide ready-made answers and conclusions for each case of investigation, because 'performance is unique unto itself within every culture', and its nature is 'culture- and community-specific' (Abrahams, 1975: 25; Bauman, 1975: 294; Behague, 1984: 5). It is the peculiarity of material which should determine the choice of analytical methods and theoretical approaches, as well as stimulate their extension and refinement.

Consistent with this point of view is the aim of this chapter, which is, while applying the ideas guiding research on performance practice to the analysis of Nenets song, to focus on the unique state of the performance tradition in terms of its social space, pragmatics, and relationship with the past and the present.

Singing in privacy and coping with crisis

While observing performance we naturally pay attention and often become attracted to the individual features of expression. Yet there is more to every performance than its idiosyncrasies. Each tradition of performance practice has its own pattern, and every individual within the tradition follows the pattern, despite variations produced by many individual behaviours.

The first thing you learn about the Nenets while in the tundra is that they are shy, quiet, and seemingly passive individuals. This image, however, drastically changes the moment they start to sing. As soon as the urging toward expression bursts out into melodic and rhythmic flow of speech, every Nenets turns into a passionate, emotionally generous personality, who has an intense and interesting inner world to share. Everything in the world of the song is unlike the everyday world, especially song characters, who struggle to overcome some incredible obstacles to success and freedom.

Such intense periods of heightened activity are natural experiences for the Nenets, and they may last for hours (in the past they could last for entire days and nights). In the Nenets communities, singing is more like a mode of life rather than a staged or framed behaviour. The people certainly do not regard the performances as work which should be rewarded; the idea of asking for monetary compensation for these sometimes very exhausting performances never seems to cross their mind.

For every Nenets to be able to express him/herself through song while alone is a necessity. The solitary type of song performance, popular among the Nenets, lies at the core of their performance practice. Public performances take the form of small concerts in front of a limited circle of family members and neighbours. Since both performer and audience share the same level of musical competence, the presence of the audience does not distract from the intimate atmosphere of the music. On such occasions, the singers still behave as if they are singing for themselves, deeply immersed in the performance, as if possessed by the characters and events of the stories, and those who are listening join the singers in their experiences.

The general characteristics described above show a pattern which characterizes the Nenets' song performance practice as essentially a private phenomenon isolated from official meddling and ideological influence.[6] In effect the Nenets are hiding the cultural traditions which are so important to them, in order to protect them from external pressures. Private song performance becomes a means of reliving the past, a way of recreating the pre-Soviet identity of the Nenets. Singing gives them confidence, as well as sense of security and comfort which the present world does not provide for them.

In fact, Soviet officials never threatened the private practice of song performances. They prohibited and completely eliminated only the public forms of musical activities exercised by professional shamans. Yet the destruction of shamanism as a social institution did not lead the Nenets to abandon their beliefs. As ethnographers discovered at the beginning of the 20th century (Joki, 1978: 384), the shamanistic beliefs of the Samoyed were not weakened either by Christian missionaries nor by Soviet officials. Nevertheless, Soviet political aggression did take its toll. A Lapp legend describes a macabre picture reflecting the tragedy of this social transition – a communal suicide of Lapp shamans.

> [W]hen they realized that their time was over, they went at night to a river bank and together indulged in a session of ecstatic singing. Next morning seven of them were found lifeless on the river's edge with their legs hanging in the water (Emsheimer, 1991a: 129).

Usually, however, traditional religious communities resorted to less radical forms and strategies of resistance. Yet all of them were mourning their past.

The oppression of native spirituality created a conflict between the inner and outer realities of the people, and had a dramatic effect on their behaviour. The quiet, suppressed, and passive manner of the Nenets population, as well as the widespread alcoholism, were the signs of a social depression and the people's denial of the new reality that faced them. To live through this conflict many of the northern peoples put up an invisible demarcation line between their official social life and personal life. Thus, ironically, the strenuous efforts of the intruders to destroy the native cultures gave the peoples 'all the more reason to cling to their beliefs and with them their songs' (Cushing, 1981: 228).

The success of this strategy was in large part due to one of the features of the Nenets' song tradition. Even in pre-Soviet times, the natural settings for the Nenets to perform their songs were either alone in the desert, or at home with their families. The notes of fieldworkers who observed the song performances when shamanism was still in existence reveal an introspective, inward-oriented performance behaviour, not necessarily requiring public exposure or involvement in shamanic seances. Castren, Donner, Shirokogoroff, as well as other scholars, have written about the detachment of the performers from reality, as indicated by their frozen posture, and the dream-trance-like style of their improvisations. Although this manner of performance was usually associated with the shamans, it was also typical for singers who did not have the professional shamans' duties.

The same introspective manner of musical behaviour was characteristic of the performers I heard in the Soviet Nenets settlements, where neither shamans nor shamanic seances seemed to exist anymore. The fact that the characteristics of the song performances in the post-shamanistic Nenets society match the descriptions of the performance behaviour in the past points to the widely discussed problem of the relation between the folk song traditions of the northern peoples and their religious practices and beliefs known as shamanism.

Multiple identity: shaman-poet-singer

The confluence of shamans with the artistic traditions of their nations was mentioned by ethnographers who witnessed shamanism alive (Bogoraz-Tan, 1910; Anuchin, 1914). In various folk traditions, deep self-absorption and outstanding artistic skills characterizing performers were often regarded as signs of shamanic gift and inspiration, but there were no specific terms separating the religious and artistic functions of musical performances (Vasilevich, 1959: 157-8). Among the Reindeer Tungus of Transbaikalia, for example, the shaman was called *oyovun* or *nordjarifki* (*nordojari* means to sing), the one who was both praying and singing (Shirokogoroff, 1935: 378).

The shaman-artist-singer compound identity is also found in the plots of epic stories which feature characters who combine cultic and artistic functions. Victor Zhirmunsky points out the similarities between the healing and charismatic abilities of the national epic singer-heroes like Väinämöinen, Baian, Alpamysh who have the magic skills typical of shamans (Chadwick and Zhirmunsky, 1969: 332-4). He refers to the folk belief that the 'art of poetry is a mysterious gift bestowed on the person by a prophetic call from on high,' just as a calling of a shaman is deemed to be bestowed by a higher authority. Finally, he devotes a special study to the shamanic identity of epic bards (Zhirmunsky, 1979).

Hatto contemplates the multiple identity of the shaman-poet-singer as well. He illustrates the inseparability of epic traditions and shamanic spirituality by a number of ethnic examples, ranging from the Sumerian Gilgamesh to the *hauki* of the Ainu living on Sakhalin Island. Looking for 'any connections there may be between shamanism and epic poetry', Hatto finds the traces of shamanism not only in the content of narratives, but in the 'heightened perception conveyed through first personal narration', and in the 'excitement bordering on ecstasy' (Hatto, 1970).

Stylistic uniformity between shamanic and other folk genres reinforces the idea of shaman-artist identity. Hajdu discovers the principle of relationship between words and melody typical of all Nenets songs, including the songs of shamans (Hajdu, 1978). Novik points out the integration of folklore and religion by revealing a structural isomorphism between narrative and shamanistic ritual (Novik, 1984; 1990). The hypothesis of a codified sacred language which in the past was used by hunters, shamans, and singers alike strengthens the notion of the extremely homogeneous symbolic communication unifying shamans with common people (Bogoraz-Tan, 1919; Revunenkova, 1980: 41).

Thus, despite the existence of misleading dichotomies, such as art versus religion, artist versus shaman, there is overwhelming evidence from different cultures confirming the association of musical performances with magic and shamanism. Because Western culture tends to differentiate between professional occupations and cultural pursuites (e.g. doctors or priests, artists or scientists), scholars have spent much time trying to solve the 'chicken and egg' kind of problem: which comes first, artist or shaman, epics or shamanism?

Some scholars were cautious, arguing that epics had numerous origins (Hatto, 1970: 19), others adhered to a more narrow view that shamans borrowed songs from the people (Vasilevich, 1959: 153), or to the contrary, that the people learned the songs from shamans (Revunenkova, 1984: 34). Emsheimer initially believed that 'the predecessors of the epic singers ... were shamans' (Emsheimer, 1970: 360). But in a later work he changed his mind.

> I expressed the view that the epic poetry grew out of the shamanic poetry. Today I am of another opinion. ... [T]he epics ... developed in early historical times out of the deep stratum of a game-hunting way of life. We may assume that these epics were taken over by the shamans and were modified, transformed and adapted by them to their cosmological world view (Emsheimer, 1991b: 154-5).

However, in view of the extreme integration and syncretism of the shamanistic cultures of Eurasia and Siberia, the debate on the origin of shaman or artist loses its meaning. Why should we keep trying to disentangle an undifferentiated homogeneous whole, if we can find a more realistic concept to define its complexity?

The amalgamation of the shaman and artist becomes more understandable in historical perspective. There are two keys to a better understanding of this identity: (1) the existence of a so-called 'family shamanism', 'democratized shamanism', or 'general inspirational shamanism'; and (2) the historical dynamics of shamanism, the process of specialization and professionalization which led to the emergence of the professional class of shamans in the past.

The term 'democratized shamanism' defines the polyfunctional oneness of religious and cultural practices and experiences, in which every person in society may participate. Before the shaman as a spiritual leader, religious specialist, or professional actor was singled out among the people, every individual could shamanize and display the skills and techniques which later became the shaman's professional monopoly.

The signs of democratized shamanism have been registered in different shamanistic regions: among the Chukchee (Bogoraz-Tan, 1904-10), the American Indians (Lowie, 1934: 312), the Lapps (Skanke, 1943: 222), the Tungus (Shirokogoroff, 1935), and other peoples. As Shirokogoroff points out:

> [t]he function of the shamans as accumulators of knowledge should not be taken as a professional function. Every Tungus may do this, and every Tungus may be interested in shamanism (Shirokogoroff, 1935: 376).

In the light of these discoveries it becomes clear that shamans did not invent the tradition by themselves, rather they inherited it from previous generations like everything else in these societies.

As a result of a gradually increasing specialization and social differentiation in the shamanistic societies, the exclusive social function of shaman-professionals did emerge, and the most talented personalities began to specialize in doing better what the general population had always done anyway. Shamans utilized the widespread religious and artistic unity, and adjusted it to the goals of their social institution. The fact that the song tradition continues without the shamanistic professional establishment proves this to be true.

Thus, the Nenets' song has become an integral and most enduring aspect of folk shamanism, the perpetual stronghold of the entire traditional culture.

Existing *before* and *along with* the professional shamanism, it now provides a relief and comfort for the people *after* the social institution has been destroyed.

A recent study on Arctic adaptation criticizes a previously held view of the traditional societies in this geographical area as static, conservative, and lacking potential for future development. The author emphasizes change taking place in the nomadic societies, which has contributed to the adaptation of the northern peoples to the Arctic environment (Krupnik, 1989; 1993). The dynamics of the Nenets' song tradition is a part of the cultural dynamics. The ability of the people to adjust their ideological and artistic strategies to changing social conditions has been one of many other factors securing the psychological survival and adaptation of the nation.

In our time, when 'shamanism stands at historic and paradoxical crossroads', being 'endangered in many of its native homelands', or 'becoming popular, even faddishly so, in the West' (Walsh, 1990: 264), the Nenets people relive their shamanistic culture in their unique way. They neither compete with nor confront any other religions with their views (Thomas and Humphrey, 1994: 11), nor are they able to observe them as a fully functioning political-religious system (Santos-Granero, 1991: 1). Instead, they find a natural and modest solution of sustaining and re-experiencing their culture through song in the private domain of their lives.

The historical dimension of the performance/context relationship

The blanket term 'context' disguises a multiplicity of specific interconnections between musical performance and environment which stretch in various directions in both time and space.

The performances of Nenets songs, to a large extent, are the moments of the people's celebration of the past, a means of their identifying themselves with previous generations and traditional values. Therefore, the invisible traditional social context is as important for our comprehension of the people and their songs as the social context observable in the present.

As our field observations suggest, the ties of the Nenets' song with their traditional culture, which prevail on both its psychological and stylistic levels, become crucial for understanding the Nenets' song tradition. This does not mean that the present conditions have no role to play in the performances. Depending on the performing situation and its momentum, Nenets singers may experience inspirations of different depths which are then translated into the song improvisations. Both the cause and meaning of the experiences, therefore, reside in the present. But the conditions peculiar to current performance situations should not disguise the fact that there existed a socio-cultural context which brought this performing practice to life. Except for instantaneously emerging variations, the overall style and performance competence shared by the people has nothing to do with their current way of life. The logic of Nenets musical thought as well as the poetic system of the songs were developed long ago in a completely different social and cultural environment. All song performances of the Nenets fluctuate within one and the same traditional system of musical expression rooted in the socio-cultural context of the past. Although observation of the performances in their natural setting does help to track down the spatial 'bridges' between the music and its immediate context, it hardly allows us to reconstruct the historical connections between the songs' musical system and the traditional culture. In order to map out these historical connections, we need to depart from discussing the behavioural aspects of the performances, and look deeper into the sound structure of the songs.

The task of exploring the socio-cultural context of musical sound organization is the least elaborated area of ethnomusicological analysis.

> [W]hile recognizing the contention of numerous scholars in ethnomusicology that the social context of a composition or a piece is not external to its music sound-structure, we must confess that our analytical tools for establishing that relationship unequivocally lack in sophistication (Behague, 1984: 8).

In spite of all the pitfalls of structural analysis, I resort to it for the sake of revealing the intimate relationship of the Nenets' song with their vanished traditional culture. The goal of the next chapter is to prepare the structural data for such an interpretation.

Notes

1. Nenets song-*khynnabts* (Kupriianova, 1960: 255; 1965: 21-2).
2. Nar'ian Mar is the administrative centre of the Nenets Autonomous National District which is a part of the Archangel province of Russia.
3. Once, I knocked on the door of Maria Iavtycaia's house in Nel'min Nos. Nobody answered, yet I could hear a singing voice. Since the Nenets never locked their doors, I took the liberty of entering the house. I saw a woman sitting on a bed deeply immersed in singing. Her only listener was a cat in a corner of the room. The woman paid no attention to me or my tape-recorder. When she finished, I tried to talk to her, but she was indifferent, and completely detached from reality. Such intriguing behaviour provokes a question: if music is a means of communication, then whom do the people who sing to themselves communicate with – the Invisible, the Beyond, or maybe a cat or reindeer?

4. Among various Arctic peoples it was common that 'man, or rather some men, somehow can break away from their immediate surroundings, even from themselves', in order to 'find the road', and develop their power of exploring an inner spiritual world (Christiansen, 1953: 29). Knut Rasmussen gave an example of a shaman's confession, which was almost identical with the Tikhon Apitsin's memory of a crisis he had in his childhood. An Eskimo shaman (*angekok*) described his passing through that crisis: 'Then I sought solitude, and here I soon became very melancholy. I would sometimes fall to weeping and feel unhappy without knowing why. Then for no reason, all would suddenly be changed, and I felt a great inexplicable joy, so powerful that I could not restrain it, but had to break into song, a mighty song, with only room for the one word: joy, joy!' (Rasmussen, 1929: 118-19).
5. The terms 'little' and 'great' were used by M. Singer to define the folk and art musical traditions, respectively, of South Asia (Singer, 1972).
6. If the private versus public characters of song performance practices in the world were put on a continuum, the Nenets' song tradition would take place at the extreme private point of such a continuum. An opposite position would be occupied by the performance practice among Aymara in Southern Peru, where 'musical performance is a group activity that takes place almost exclusively in public-community fiesta contexts', and where men 'rarely perform music alone in private'. Quite contrary to the Nenets, they view private musical performance as 'odd behavior', which they cannot understand (Turino, 1989: 10).

CHAPTER THREE

The Structure of the Song: Poetical and Musical Texts

Rhythm: ...
Escape from Logic ...
Confluence with Name ...
Archaic ... Multidimensional Sign.[1]

Nenets song as a complex structural whole

As a sound symbolic system integrating language and music, song constitutes an enormous complexity. There are three basic structural systems comprising song: (1) the linguistic system of speech; (2) the 'secondary modeling system' (Lotman, 1977: 9), or the system of poetic and literary-fictional norms superimposed on speech; and (3) the system of musical thought, which embraces all other parallel distributed systems with 'harmony and grace' (Zhirmunsky, 1975: 439).

Each of the systems has its own stratification. A number of subordinate linguistic systems, each carrying its own functions and meanings, coexist in language. According to the theory of stratificational grammar (Lamb, 1966: 1), natural language has six strata. Each of its three major componental systems – semology, grammar and phonology – splits into two additional strata. All the strata cannot ideally correspond with each other, and thus structural discrepancies and asynchronical combinations become inevitable.

> One of the reasons for the complexity of linguistic structure, i.e. for the fact that it comprises several stratal systems rather than just one or two, is that *sounds and meanings are, by their natures, patterned separately from each other*; they each have their own structural relationships. Phonological systems must be adapted to the articulatory and auditory organs, while semiological systems must be adapted to thought patterns (Lamb, 1966: 2).

A further level of stratification occurs when the issue of speech intonation enters the equation. Usually, linguists characterize intonation as a paralinguistic phenomenon existing on the surface of language relatively independently, since intonation forms its own structural and semantic units, not always synchronized with those of language (Svetozarova, 1982: 24). The contradictions between linguistic units of speech and the logic of intonation seem to be normal for both everyday and artistic speech (Tedlock, 1990: 135-6; Hymes, 1977: 453-4).

Forms of rhetoric, such as narrative and poetry, add more strata to the growing 'pyramid' of verbal expression, thus structural discrepancies and contradictions between all the strata become even more conspicuous. Narrative semiotics considers all narrative texts, both oral and literary, as complex systems which are built upon language, and which split into additional structural strata parallel to those of language. Various semiotic theories define the constituent interdependent strata in different terms. Denotative and connotative planes of the texts refer to the levels of linguistic form and non-linguistic substance, respectively. Each of the two fundamental levels splits further into its own levels of *apparent* expression and *immanent* content, into *signifying* and *signified* (in Saussure's terms), or into *surface* and *deep* structures (in Chomsky's terms).

The superimposition of poetical rhythm and syntax on linguistic and narrative complexes introduces an extra system of expression and content, which complements the complexity, already highly meaningful and stratified. Additional non-correspondences and structural discrepancies emerge, such as the clash between speech and poetic syntaxes, or between words and poetic rhythm. Rhythm unifies and blurs the boundaries between linguistic units but it also adds more to the asynchrony of the linear subsystems. 'The intentional discrepancy' between metrical and syntactic divisions in poetic structure has been discussed by Roman Jakobson and other scholars (Jakobson, 1960: 367; Drogalina and Nalimov, 1978; Zhinkin, 1965).

Song is the next level of the structural complexity. The stratification and asynchrony of the parallel componental structural systems in song is much more dense than in speech or poetry. While melody in poetry is present only tacitly, in song it exists as a full-fledged highly differentiated sound system based, mainly, on pitch, rhythm, and form organization.

The most difficult aspect of melody, usually escaping categorization, is its *immanent* level, or semantics. As one and the same melody allows for innumerable juxtapositions of words with different meanings, its own meaning becomes an infinite, immeasurable and unpredictable continuum of interpretations. It always 'turns over to the interpreter the right to complete the determination as he pleases' (Sebeok, 1977: ix).

This excursion into the depth of song form's stratification aims at highlighting the complexity and density underlying the creation and performance of song. Although the following analysis of the structural system of Nenets song cannot be incremental to the same extent, the awareness of the range of the structural complexity of song, I hope, enhances my more general approach.

Before I attempt to extract the melodic system of Nenets song from this complexity and look at it in relation to other complementary systems, linguistic and poetic, I must first review what linguists and philologists have learned about Nenets song.

Language

There is unanimity among scholars studying colloquial Nenets and the language of Nenets folklore that both systems are extremely homogeneous. Territorial differences are so minimal that they can hardly be qualified as dialectal.

> Despite the vast territory of the people's distribution, their language is in all respects uniform. Even the people living in the opposite parts of the tundra understand each other without any difficulty. Some divergencies occur at the level of phonetics, but they do not touch upon the basic phonological structure of the language. There is no significant difference in the grammar, neither in its morphology, nor in its syntax. Some minor territorial distinctions in the vocabulary are limited only to the manner of pronunciation (Tereshchenko, 1990: 7).

Tereshchenko observes the same degree of structural uniformity in the language of all Nenets folklore genres. Formulaic expressions distinguishing Nenets poetic language from colloquial speech cut across different regional folklore genres (Tereshchenko, 1980: 41-6).

Hajdu confirms the ubiquity of verbal formulas, 'more or less fixed phrases', and 'set expressions', which characterize the national poetic style. Meaningless syllables, insertions and expletives emerge in the poetic language of the songs, no matter when and where the people sing their songs. Extrapolating these features discovered in Nenets shamanic songs to other song genres of the Nenets' folklore, Hajdu recognizes the structural uniformity of the poetic language throughout different locales and different genres of the song tradition.

> The study of the songs sung by the Nenets shaman ... cannot for the present be separated from that of other works of folk poetry ... both lyric and epic poetry (Hajdu, 1978: 355).

He also invites attention to an interesting phenomenon, which is the intrusion of peculiar elements of the song poetic language into the peoples' everyday speech, indicative of the important role of song in the Nenets' culture.

> Our knowledge of the language of song may then elucidate phenomena which have puzzled us so far. Some word forms have morphemic variants which are not recorded in grammar books. These forms took shape in singing, from where they found their way into colloquial speech and created new morphemic variants (Hajdu, 1978: 366).

The musically based structure of the poetic language, so thoroughly analyzed by Hajdu, represents the pattern of melody/word relationship typical of Nenets song, which is characterized by the structural superiority of melody over verbal thought.

Mimesis

The fictional world of the Nenets' song poetry has its own conventions pertaining to how it models reality. The increasing knowledge of the Nenets about their environment and new social experiences led to developing a certain diversity of poetic genre-models classified in different ways by philologists and by the people themselves. Although there are several scholarly genre classifications of Nenets songs, each of them distinguishes three basic categories: shamanic, epic, and lyric songs. Some overlap between the categories occurs, however, when a shaman, for example, performs an epic song, or when a song has both epic and lyric characteristics. Obviously, actual performance tends to resist the rigidity of any classifications.

The native typology of Nenets song follows a different logic. An elaborate song terminology used by the people has none of the three scholarly song categories mentioned above. For example, there is no native concept of shamanic song, which is unsurprising as Nenets shamans used to share one and the same song tradition with the rest of the people (see pp. 39-42). Also unsurprising is the lack of the other two philological categories of song – the epic and lyrical song categories, because they are both products of comparative cross-cultural analysis of folk songs. These two 'universal' categories could hardly have been created by analytical thinking from within a single culture.

Let us now associate the native categories of song with what the people actually create, in order to see which particular aspect of Nenets song is reflected in each category.

The broadest category in the Nenets' native song terminology is *iangebts* (*iangeb* means 'to sing'). It signifies anything which is meant to be sung. The concept emphasizes musical performance of any verbal text, and separates song as a unity of words and melody, in principle, from all unsung genres called *vadako* (word), and including, for example, among other *vadako* types, *lakhanako* (tale).

The term *khynnabts* encompasses all Nenets songs. It defines specifically Nenets song as opposed to the songs of other peoples. This concept refers to that set of structural characteristics which underlies every genre category of Nenets song, and therefore, constitutes the conventional stereotype of the whole song tradition.

In place of the scholarly category of epic song the people have two separate concepts – *siudbabts* and *iarabts*, which specify the different types of narrative developed within the epic tradition (see Appendix for examples).

Each of the two categories of Nenets epic song has its peculiar themes, characters, images and expressions, but there is one plot pattern underlying both of the categories. The pattern is a long chain of slowly changing episodes, not necessarily directly connected with one another. The narratives start with an introduction or exposition of the characters and their situations. There then follows the hero's departure on a distant and risky journey. After many dangerous adventures and victories, the hero returns back home. What distinguishes the epic plots as heroic, as opposed to magic plots, is that the heroes win by strength, rather than by supernatural forces.

Siudbabts is the oldest type of Nenets heroic epic. Its content reflects the structure and lifestyle of the tribal, pre-feudal society. *Siudbia* is a giant, a monster and a cruel cannibal. A confrontation between the human-hunting giant and the hero is at the core of all *siudbabts*' plots. The resolution is always the same: despite the giant's strength, the hero wins because he is smarter. There exist a few stereotypical *siudbabts* themes: a dangerous journey aimed at finding a wife in a distant land, a bloody revenge for a murdered family member, and a struggle for reindeer herds. The three themes often intertwine in one song.

The ideals and values of the Nenets clan stand behind every theme and event taking place in *siudbabts*' plots. The dangerous task of looking for a wife far away from home is the responsibility of the whole clan, which usually supports the hero and accompanies him on his journey. The theme reflects the law of exogamic marriage, which used to be strong and indeed obligatory among the Nenets. A bloody revenge for a murder used to be a law of the tribal society as well. It reflected the basic concern of the people with the continuity of their clan. The people symbolized their belief in continuity by the image of the hearth which they had to constantly keep up, never allowing it to burn out.

Siudbabts features a third-person narrative. The narrator is very often 'Song' itself. The formulaic expressions connecting one episode with another portray the animated character of Song. Here is an example of a typical start to a *siudbabts*.

> Once upon a time, Song found a home on a river bank.
> An old woman lived in this house with her two children:
> a ten-year-old daughter and a seven-year-old son.
> Nobody visited them, and nobody left them for three years.
> After the three years had passed, Song told them:
> 'Look, there is a stranger coming to you
> on two graceful reindeer-bulls!'
> Song recognized the stranger:
> 'It is Khan Khadengota who is coming to you!'
> (Kupriianova, 1965: 122)

Descriptions and comparisons in *siudbabts* are typically hyperboles exaggerating almost every aspect of the story: the events and situations, the strength of the hero, time and space. The plots are schematic and lack dialogue. The characters are described only by their actions, rather than by feelings and thoughts.

As a result of the increasing role of personality and individual consciousness in the tribal society, a lyrical quality was brought into Nenets epic, which led to the emergence of the type of narrative called *iarabts*. The *iarabts* include more detailed descriptions of situations and landscapes, as well as expressions of the people's feelings. The typical epic themes of the distant journey, bloody revenge, and the struggle for deer herds are less fantastic, enhanced by realistic details about the characters' everyday lives.

Literally, *iarabts* means a lament. The verb *iart'* means to lament the poor and unhappy destiny of a suffering and struggling individual, usually an orphan-boy. Humiliated and abused, the boy often wants to die. The description of his suffering becomes the crux of the *iarabts* stories. The emphasis on the inner feelings of the hero changes the epic narrative to such an extent that it is no longer an impersonal third-person narrative, but an emotionally touching first-person monologue by the hero himself.

Iarabts stories share with *siudbabts* the same type of composition, the same thematic formulas, and utilize the same stock of stereotypical expressions. Despite their differences, the two types of Nenets epic song are based on the same general model, and fulfil one and the same function in the Nenets' traditional society. Although, the people do not identify this function by a special term, which would subsume *siudbabts* and *iarabts* under one epic genre category, they do allot to both types of songs that extraordinary status which is universally associated with the function of epics.

The epic stories, whether they are *siudbabts* or *iarabts*, play an exclusive role in the Nenets' culture, since they reflect the people's ideals and values, and commemorate their history. The people view all epic stories seriously, as if the characters really existed and the events really happened. They also show a great respect for those who perform the songs.

Besides the epic, there is another popular type of song in the Nenets' culture, which can be defined as song of solitude. The need to sing to themselves is strong among the Nenets. A person can start singing while alone in the tundra: riding a deer, boating, or making crafts. There is no pattern for the themes and images contained in the solitude song. Anything that a person may see, feel, or think can be poeticized and transformed into a song. Philologists define the lyrical song as improvisatory, as opposed to the epic plots developing according to a certain formula. Indeed, the variety of the contents and performance situations among lyrical songs resists classification. The people themselves differentiate between the songs by means of the adjectives they add to the noun *sio* (voice) – *natseky sio*: children's song, *yabe sio*: drunk song, etc.

Despite the variety of contents, the lyrical songs follow the uniform structural pattern typical for all Nenets songs. So far, the pattern has been briefly defined as the melody/word type of relationship characterized by the structural prevalence of melody over words (see p. 48), and it will be described in more detail in the next chapter. The uniformity is covered by the native category *khynnabts*, meaning the Nenets' national song in general.

Nenets everywhere show no preference for any particular genre. The whole set of song genres[2] is equally popular among performers living in different places of the Nenets tundra.

The melodic system

The Nenets' musical style is analysed here as a system of structural principles restraining musical communication within the national community. The analysis is based mainly on my own field recordings, but it takes into account song recordings by other collectors as well. I listened to Shcherbakova's collection stored in the phonogram archives of the Pushkin House in St Petersburg and Bogdanov's collection stored in the archives of the Union of the Soviet Composers in Moscow. All published musical transcriptions of Nenets songs were also examined (Väisänen, 1965; Dobrovol'sky, 1965; Vakhitova, 1988). As a result, I discovered that the stylistic features pertinent to the songs which I recorded myself also characterize the songs in other collections.

The scope of the mentioned musical data does not cover all manifestations of the Nenets' song tradition. Often, collectors selected the places and singers for observation and recordings haphazardly. Nevertheless, the accumulated material provides quite sufficient evidence for some generalizations.[3]

The settlement of the nomadic people into stable villages enabled the Nenets' song collectors to observe various stylistic patterns while working at a single location. Nenets families, having wandered over different parts of the tundra before gathering together in a village community, brought with them song traditions from various regions. It seems reasonable to assume that if the different melodic styles concentrated at one settlement show some similar characteristics, these similarities are likely to be representative of the Nenets' melodic style in general.

The goal of the following analysis of melodic style is to extract from the song repertories those features which are systematic. We can hardly evaluate or explain individual properties of a concrete performance without knowing the structural system which simultaneously constrains and gives some space to individual creativity. Any change taking place in the structural characteristics of each individual performance is always combined with an underlying stability of melodic style and form.

Below I attempt to reveal the dynamic pattern of the creative process of Nenets song: the unique proportion between stability and change which distinguishes the Nenets' general melodic style as much as every individual style, or single performance.

Diversity

Nenets melody is, typically, a laconic solo 'sentence' which singers reiterate for hours or, as was common in the past, for days. During the course of its repetitions the melody may change its dynamics, tempo, key, range, switch from a monophonic to a bi- or triphonic texture, but rarely changes its rhythmic design.

The most impressive feature characterizing all Nenets song performances is the proliferation of melodic ideas, which seem to be inexhaustible. I never heard two singers use the same melody, or one singer use the same melody twice, but I heard singers switching to a second melody during lengthy performances. This melodic diversity characterized the song repertories recorded at both Nel'min Nos and Indiga. Each of the melodies displayed its own distinctive rhythmic design and melodic contour.[4]

3.1 A. Vyucheisky, Nel'min Nos

3.2 A. Vyucheisky, Nel'min Nos

3.3 N. Taleieva, Nel'min Nos

3.4 N. Taleieva, Nel'min Nos

3.5 U. Apitsina, Indiga

3.6 M. Iavtysaia, Nel'min Nos

3.7 M. Argeieva, Indiga

3.8 F. Belugin, Indiga

3.9 F. Belugin, Indiga

3.10 F. Belugin, Indiga

3.11 F. Belugin, Indiga

3.12 S. Apitsin

3.13 S. Apitsin

3.14 S. Apitsin

3.15 Ie. Belugina, Indiga

3.16 Ie. Belugina, Indiga

3.17 Ie. Belugina, Indiga

3.18 Ie. Belugina, Indiga

3.19 Ie. Belugina, Indiga

All the published musical transcriptions of Nenets songs feature the same proliferation of melodic ideas (Väisänen, 1965; Dobrovol'sky, 1965; Vakhitova, 1988).

The dominance of musical rhythm

The melodic diversity accumulated within the Nenets' song tradition is due to the extraordinary rhythmic inventiveness of Nenets singers. Almost every song performance turns into a discovery of some new rhythmic idea marking the song with its own melodical identity. A slight change in rhythm may produce different yet obviously related melodies.

3.20 S. Apitsin, Indiga

3.21 S. Apitsin, Indiga

3.22 S. Apitsin, Indiga

Even recitative melodies with a narrow range, sounding almost like speech, have their unique rhythmic configurations. The urge for rhythmic creativity is so strong among Nenets singers that I never encountered a Nenets melody imitating speech intonation and following syllabic rhythm as closely as might an epic or lament melody in other peoples' vocal traditions. Every melody has an explicit personality due to its individual rhythmic concept which does not reappear in any other song.

The dominance of musical rhythm over words in Nenets songs was noticed first by Lehtisalo who pointed out the musical origin of the poetic structure.

> The Yurak Samoyedic songs have metre only when being sung. For the lines to reach the set length, to be adjusted to the melodic curve, vowels may be lengthened into two syllables, meaningless expletive particles may be added to word endings or even inserted between syllables, and some words already uttered may be chanted anew (Lehtisalo, 1922: 84).

Later Hajdu discussed this type of melody-word relationship in more detail. He analysed the influence of musical rhythm on poetic structure and verbal formulas. At first, he focused on shaman songs, but found the same principle applied to all other sung genres of Nenets folklore. Hajdu described how the linking of the words to melodic rhythms was done.

> Expletive syllables or sounds – which play no kind of semantic, logical or grammatical part – are added to line-endings, or inserted between words ... or even between syllables. They have merely a rhythmic-metrical function, ... make possible the fusion of the basic text and the melodic pattern, synthesize text and melody (Hajdu, 1978: 357).

Since the meaningless syllables spread among and inside the song words supplied the verbal texts with a unique poetic quality, Hajdu asserted their importance for understanding the style and the meaning of the songs, and criticized the practice of publishing only the 'basic texts' of the songs which gave the contents of the poetic texts, but omitted these structural peculiarities. Hajdu's comparison of the song texts which were actually performed with these edited 'basic texts' helped to clarify the significant role of musical rhythm in Nenets song (Hajdu, 1978: 354).

Tirada: the iterative musical form

The typical Nenets melody is a concise musical statement confirmed and reinforced throughout its numerous repetitions. Most often, it consists of the main and concluding motives. An occasional introductory exclamation may lead to a core melodic idea which almost immediately comes to an ending.

The principle of repetition is crucial for the overall structure of song. The persistent repetitions of melody mould the words of song into poetic lines, and the reiterated melody becomes the actual instrument of versification.

In the unwritten folk song traditions, the poetic form of the songs' verbal texts emerges and becomes audible during performance. It can be visualized only when a transcription takes into account the musical form of the songs. But when the verbal text of a folk song is transcribed without considering the melodic repetitions, it looks like prose. Criticizing such inadequate graphical representations of Nenets songs, Hajdu shows the differences between the non-musical and musical approaches to textualization. I illustrate the two approaches by the two transcriptions of a Nenets song text. The first transcription looks like prose because it disregards the iterative form of the song melody, but when the same text is rendered in accordance with its musical form, it acquires a peculiar poetic shape, showing how the melody's repetitions divide the flow of the words into verses as well as larger units comprising groups of verses.[5]

Мане нисями вэсако си'ми' вадавые, тенаней тяхадэй, сэванэй тяхадэй. Вадабата подэй', нодэй' небянэ-нисянэй' мэвые таняно,нэми'таня' нивыэ'. Манедэй, эмане хав(а)нане' папавэй таняно - Сидя Ламдивэця. /Сидя Ламдивэця, ма'нив, папав таня./ Мане тэри мак(а)вава', ма'нив,нока вуни танё', ма'нив,-си'ив ю'мя'нэва', ма'нив,-тынэ пэрэна'мов, (ма'нив).

3.23a A. Vyucheisky, Nel'min Nos

Мане нисями вэсако си'ми' вадавые, тенаней тяхадэй,
сэванэй тяхадэй. Вадабата подэй', нодэй'
небянэ-нисянэй' мэвые таняно,
нэми'таня' нивыэ'.
Манедэй, эмане хав(а)нане' папавэй таняно - Сидя Ламдивэця.
/Сидя Ламдивэця, ма'нив, папав таня./
Мане тэри мак(а)вава', ма'нив, нока вуни танё', ма'нив, -си'ивю'мя'нэва',
ма'нив, -тынэ пэрэна'мов, (ма'нив).

3.23b A. Vyucheisky, Nel'min Nos

3.23c A. Vyucheisky, Nel'min Nos

The musical transcription of the song (3.23c) visualizes the persistent reiterations of melody, or that 'fairly rigid form' which Albert Lord defines as a structural framework for epic stories (Lord, 1960: 21). The form is associated with a wide range of folk genres – laments, incantations, prayers – but it is most often mentioned as a universal feature of various epic traditions in the world.

Studying the systems of versification in the epic traditions of Central Asia, Victor Zhirmunsky defined the form by the term *tirada*. He characterized *tirada* by the 'rhythmic-syntactic parallelism of consecutive verse lines', 'as regards both sense and grammar' (Zhirmunsky, 1964; Chadwick and Zhirmunsky, 1969). Compared to a song *stanza,* which consists of a fixed number of poetic lines organized into a unit, tirada has a 'stretchable' size and comprises a flexible and changeable number of verses. Since the 'rigidity' of tirada form is less than that of stanza form, there is more room left for improvisation by the performer, who is free to repeat as many verses as needed to cover a portion of an epic story.

Most typical of Nenets songs is a tirada with regular and isorhythmic repetitions of melody. This type of tirada characterizes Nenets songs with various contents and functions, and it can be found in all Nenets territories. Encountered more rarely is a tirada with irregular repetitions of melody, in which the melody may slightly change its length, but rarely the core rhythmic idea.

A larger melodic unit emerges, when a singer consistently makes a slight change in every other repetition of song melody. As a result, two melodic lines unite into a question-answer period subjected to numerous repetitions.

3.24 F. Belugin, Indiga

Expanding melody

The gradual expansion of Nenets song melody is the process of widening melodic intonations, smoothly and consistently carried out by performers through the numerous reiterations of the same melody. Although expansions are not always present in performances, they nevertheless constitute a peculiar stylistic feature of the Nenets' system of musical expression, correlated with other features already described: the rhythmic individuality of song melody and the persistence of the melody reiteration. Nenets singers resort to melody expansion only occasionally, depending on their state of mind, the ambience of the performance situation, and many other factors. The random nature of these expansions in the performance, as well as folklorists' belief that changes happening to song melody throughout its endless repetitions are of no importance, was probably one of the reasons why the remarkable structural feature was overlooked for so long (Gomon, 1980: 211). As a rule, researchers analysed only the beginnings of the songs, whereas the melodic expansions can be detected only if attention is paid to every repetition of the melody, from beginning to end.

This kind of melodic metamorphosis depends on the rhythmic foundation of the Nenets' melodic style. The rhythm of the melody never changes throughout the repetitions, providing a basis for the transformation of the interval size of melodic intonations. While retaining its initial rhythmic and motivic configuration, the melody maintains the identity of the song, despite the changing size of its melodic intonations.

Perhaps the most striking aspect of these melodic expansions is the consistency and sophistication with which Nenets performers carry out the transformation process. The following description of this process is abstracted from a number of individual performances in order to create a model.

The melodic expansions are not present at the start of the song performances. Usually there is first a series of rather exact reiterations of the melody, performed in a relaxed manner, within a comfortable voice register for the singer. The range of the melody during the exposition is relatively narrow. Sooner or later, the tendency to expand the interval size of the melodic intonations becomes noticeable. Some of the pitches begin to move up or down slightly. Most often, the expansion proceeds in the ascending direction, only rarely accompanied by some descent. But always, the interval change accumulates very gradually, consistently, and smoothly. All the sonorous qualities of the expanding melody – its ambitus, tessitura, timbre – noticeably change, but its rhythmic design, the core of its personality, remains intact.

The expansion is usually distributed over a flexible number of the melody's repetitions. Singers are free to determine the density of the melody's growth and ascent. They never, however, lose the direction and the perspective of the whole process, consistently progressing with the idea until reaching its culmination, when melodic intonations can exceed an octave in the most extreme cases.

The expansions are always reinforced through other parallel changes: increasing volume, accelerating tempo, and tightening vocal articulation. In addition, the key, or the tonal level, of the melody, moves upwards in the same gliding way as the smoothly progressed expansion of musical intervals. A similar gradually rising tonal transposition was registered during the lengthy performances of Karelian laments (Konkka and Gomon, 1977: 346).

All these means of melodic progression simultaneously employed by the singers may lead them to such heightened levels of tension and excitement, reaching the utmost limits of their physical abilities, that they become unable to continue the expansion further. At this point, the performers abruptly return to the melody's initial moderate manner of performance and range. For a while the singers remain in a relaxed state, until they feel ready to undertake the next ascent.

Elsewhere I have described the course of this melodic expansion, from the beginning to its culmination, as a 'super period' (Gomon, 1990: 83). The number of super periods carried out through the melodic reiterations is variable. It depends entirely on the emotional state and creative consciousness of the singers. The cycle of super periods, developing independently from both the tirada-like musical form and the verbal plot, forms an extra structural level of such song improvisations. How exactly asynchronical this cycle is with the narrative plot, or any other type of poetic content, is a subject for further investigation.

When executing these expansions, the singers never make conspicuous interval steps. The steps are gliding, each one being less than a quarter of a tone. The accumulation of the changes takes place over the course of many repetitions. Only after a number of repetitions does the ascent (or descent) of melodic pitches become clearly perceptible. The expansion glides smoothly through the whole scale of pitches, including those which are not available in the temperament scale. A musical transcription is capable of representing only those steps of the gliding expansion which coincide with the pitches of the temperament scale, or for which there is an appropriate line and an adequate symbol on the five-line staff. Inevitably, such notation, omitting the many intermediary repetitions in which the gliding cannot be identified with some notes, is extremely schematic. In reality, it takes a much longer time to accomplish the process than can be demonstrated by a musical example.

3.25 N. Taleieva, Nel'min Nos

3.26 Ie. Belugina, Indiga

The expanding melodies are not unique to the repertories of the singers I met in Nel'min Nos and Indiga. The Nenets performers witnessed by Finnish ethnomusicologist Jarkko Niemi in 1994 (see p. 3) also demonstrated this melodic technique.[6] Some signs of the melodic expansion can also be found at the very start of the musical transcriptions published by Väisänen (1965: nos 17, 20, 35, 37, 43).

The musical examples I have presented here testify to the important role played by the technique of melodic expansion in the Nenets' song performance. The cultural meaning and function of this and other stylistic features of the Nenets' melodies is the subject of the next chapter of this study.

The individual song styles

Every Nenets performer creates his or her own personal musical style within the restrictions of the song tradition. Individual stylistic idiosyncrasies emerge in all aspects of the songs: in the character of melodic rhythm, preferred length and phrase configuration of the repetitive melodic units, manner of executing the melodic expansions, density of the ascents, and heights of the culminations.

Each individual song style is naturally influenced by the singer's personality. For example, I am inclined to call the style of Tikhon Apitsin, a bard from Indiga, dramatic. In his repertory we can find the combination of rhetorical passionate melodies with lyrical, tender, and sad ones. He designs relatively extended melodic units including question-and-answer type melodies. His expansions unfold slowly, but consistently. To build tension he concentrates on his articulation, increasing the volume or tempo, or introducing an intense trembling quality to his voice, rather than using the most extreme ranges of expansion.

The melodies of another prolific singer from Indiga, Fiodor Belugin, have an energetic, courageous, and even militant character. Typically, they consist of two similar melodic sentences organized into a period due to a slight difference in the second sentence. His manner of executing the expansions is reserved. The ascents proceed slowly, and the melodic culminations do not reach the highest pitches, but the tension, built ever so gradually and modestly, is felt strongly.

The melodic styles of the Nenets' female singers have special characteristics. The musical themes of the women-bards are usually concise one-line melodies with a dance-like character. The melodies, however, often go through intense expansions, reaching the widest ranges and highest pitch culminations. The Nenets women get into the process of expansion very easily. They start the expansions almost from the very beginning of the song, and reach the highest points of the melodic development quite quickly. Nataliia Taleieva from Nel'min Nos and especially Iekaterina Belugina from Indiga appear to prepare themselves mentally for the emotional ascent without any difficulty or prolonged preparation. Their expansions are quite dense: the super-periods are short, the ascents accomplished quickly, and the culminations reach the highest pitches.

These individual adaptations of the songs' musical model maintain the dynamism of Nenets song tradition. As long as the musical talents of the people continue to express themselves in these ways, the renewal of the song tradition is assured.

The response of the song model to social change

Geertz has indicated that a determination to explore cultural coherence leads sometimes to a failure to recognize those aspects of culture which resist change and are incongruent with the dynamic forms of social organization (Geertz, 1957: 33). The disintegration of the typical song structure into different levels allows us to overcome this problem and see which components of the song model have responded or not responded to social change.

The elements of the song model show a different sensitivity to the social changes which took place in Nenets society. While a variety of patterns exists at the level of poetic plots and images, linguistic and musical style characteristics do not seem to be perfectly congruent with the social dynamics.

Comparison of songs from various Nenets repertories shows that there are no regional differences in the patterns of coordination between the musical form, poetic content, and social function developed in the Nenets' song tradition. The same polysemantic and polyfunctional structural model is used to serve all the plots and social functions of the musical performances.

This kind of structural stability and homogeneity is not unique to the Nenets' musical tradition. The association of one structural model with a multiplicity of contents and ritual functions exists in other folklore cultures as well. One musical form may characterize various folk genres within many national folk traditions. Among the peoples living in the Russian North, for example, vocal performances throughout an entire village, or an even larger geographical area, are often based on one melodic formula.

However, the inner dynamics of the Nenets' musical system is more complex, despite its basic homogeneity. The single structural model materializes itself in the enormous variety of melodic ideas flourishing within and across individual song repertories. Nenets singers constantly change the melodic configurations of the established song model, independently from poetic contents or performance situations. Such a high coefficient of melodic creativity constitutes the unique quality of the song tradition.

Since the prolific melodic creativity of the Nenets people is unusual and differs from the imitative way of learning typical within oral cultures, the phenomenon calls for an explanation. An answer may lie in various correlations between the musical system and the structure and ideology of traditional Nenets society.

Notes

1. Drogalina and Nalimov, 1978: 295.
2. The Nenets' classification of the song genres:

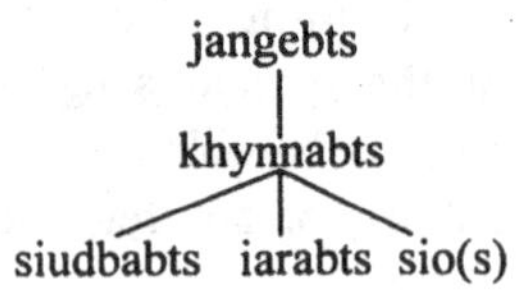

3. The generalizations can be attempted in accordance with the following heuristic rule: if there is a persistent repetition of certain features in randomly selected samples, there is a high probability that these features constitute a pattern typical of the whole tradition.
4. The following 'by-ear' notations of the tape-recorded performances were made by the author. By the nature of the task, they are approximate.
5. Example 3.23 is reprinted from Gomon, 1992: 46, 48. The prose-like transcription of the poetical text (3.23a) is made by V. Ledkov. The transcription's rearrangement (3.23b) in accordance with the song melody notation (3.23c) was made by the author.
6. Personal email communication, Spring 1995.

CHAPTER FOUR

The Historical Context of the Melodic System

> **Did the cosmologists shape their myths**
> **to account for the way music is formed, or**
> **did composers and singers shape their songs in order**
> **to make them fit a set of values promulgated in the mythology?[1]**

Traditional society

This chapter contains a socio-cultural analysis of the Nenets' melodic system. Following the previous chapters' investigations into the performance and structural aspects of the songs, it aims to move us toward a more comprehensive representation of the song tradition.

Correspondence between social and musical systems constitutes the subject of the sociology of music, which studies the social aspects of sound structure as much as those of musical behaviour in performance. The role of social factors in shaping musical sound organization has been discussed in many ethnomusicological analyses (Seeger, 1980; Becker and Becker, 1981; Feld, 1984; Behague, 1984; Nettl, 1987; 1992: 184-94), dismissing the previously held view that dealing with musical structure excludes 'social involvements', and 'social interpretations' (Mueller, 1963: 216-20).

The concept of a socio-cultural interpretation of musical styles results from the awareness that these styles are conventions established within societies, and thus are based on the peculiarities of those societies. From this primary point of view, socio-cultural analyses of music becomes a legitimate concern for both musicology and sociology.

The structuralist approach to socio-musical analysis conforms with the basic line of thinking in social science, which repeatedly postulates that the essential categories of thought 'come from society', that 'the very things they express are social' (Durkheim, 1915; 1995: 441), or, in other words, that '[h]uman thought is consummately social: social in its origins, social in its functions, social in its forms, social in its applications' (Geertz, 1966: 1).

The assumption of such mutual correspondence between musical thought organizing sound and society brings back the concept of 'Tylor's most complex whole', a subject of scepticism for quite a long time. Geertz has criticized the 'excessive popularity' of this concept, which, as he has argued, no longer has 'a grandiose, all-promising scope and the infinite versatility of apparent application' (Geertz, 1973: 4). Not denying the 'originating power' of the concept, he thinks, however, that for analyses of cultural phenomena in the modern world, the concept obscures a good deal more than it reveals.

> Nothing has done more, I think, to discredit cultural analysis than the construction of impeccable depictions of formal order in whose actual existence nobody can quite believe (Geertz, 1973: 18).

Arguing that 'coherence cannot be the major test of validity for a cultural description', Geertz, at the same time, admits that 'cultural systems must have a minimal degree of coherence', otherwise 'we would not call them systems'. The critical part of his argument states that 'by observation, they [cultural systems] normally have a great deal more' (Geertz, 1973: 17).

Geertz, therefore, understands cultural coherence as a matter of degree, which implies that the expression/context relationship may include juxtaposition of both coherent and disruptive features. In egalitarian pre-industrial societies, however, principles of coherence, integration, and homogeneity dominate in cultural expression and social interaction. Tylor's concept of culture as the complex interrelated whole is primarily applicable to the oral/aural cultures, rather than to the written ones. The traditional shamanistic cultures of Northern Eurasia are the most appropriate justifications of such a concept of culture. The same systematic compound of religious ideas underlies every manifestation of these cultural traditions. There hardly exists an experience or expression within any traditional shamanistic culture which can be understood separately from the complex cultural whole.

The Nenets' song tradition is both a manifestation and a remnant of such overwhelming cultural coherence. We can understand neither the people nor their songs, without re-establishing a coherent relationship between Nenets traditional society, world view, and song.

Let us look at how the Nenets' musical conventions, which make the song performances intelligible and communicable have been socially constructed. It is an assumption to be proved that the logical system existing beneath the surface of every musical expression, and the unique proportion of stereotypical and dynamic elements inherent in that system, emerge as a result of the interaction of individuals with external social and cultural conditions.

To look for the shaping conditions of the Nenets' musical style we must look into the historical past of the people, and find a match between their music and the existing knowledge about their vanished traditional culture.

Fortunately, the literature on shamanistic cultures, in general, is quite sufficient to make such reconstruction possible, and it compensates for the lack of observable ethnographic facts.

The method of analytical restoration of the whole from its remnant part is not a new one. Previously, the most popular object of reconstructions of shamanistic culture was the shamanic drum (Emsheimer, [1946] 1964; Prokof'ieva, 1961; Dioszegi, 1968; 1978; Potapov, 1978; Joki, 1978; Dolgikh, 1978; Basilov, 1984). Compared to the shamanic drum, which is now just a museum piece, Nenets song remains a vital, challenging, and promising object for reconstructive analysis. Looking at the songs in retrospect is consistent with the view that a musical system extracted from live performances is not 'a fixed and timeless world of essences'. It is emerging, invented 'by people as active agents in a historical process', never isolated from the conditions external to the musical domain (Bruner, 1986: 12).

Social factors determining the unity and inner diversity of the melodic system

Tereshchenko undertook research into why the Nenets language lacks significant regional peculiarities. She found that the roots of the language's structural uniformity lay in the organization and lifestyle of the nomadic society.

> The affinity of all the aspects of the Nenets tundra dialects, especially at the level of grammar and vocabulary, is probably, the result of a free communication between different groups of the tundra Nenets, who because of their nomadic way of life have been easily moving west and east, meeting with peoples from different territories (Tereshchenko, 1990: 10).

It is interesting to note that this uniformity that defines the Nenets as a nation has helped the people to maintain their nomadic lifestyle, allowing migrating or isolated communities to keep in contact more easily.

The highly uniform song tradition of the Nenets played a similar role. As with the common ideology, language and shared territory of the Nenets, song defined their national identity. Struggling to make and keep the northern land their home, the people turned to their song for various needs.

I would like to suggest a hypothesis that the nomadic way of life provided some special social conditions for melodic creativity, and helped the Nenets to accumulate an abundance of melodic re-formulations of the conventional song model. It seems to me that the extremely dynamic nature of the Nenets' musical system has been determined, basically, by three interrelated and overlapping traditional institutions: nomadic pastoralism, the society's clan organization, and the law of exogamy. These social establishments do not exist anymore, but they have left their traces in the musical system of the song tradition.

Nomadic pastoralism. The plots of Nenets epic songs reflect basic preoccupations with survival: the reindeer, mobility (the basis of their economy) and the family. The reindeer in the song stories is never a fantastic image, but plays a real part in the people's lives, often described in the song poetic texts in technical terms of the breeding economy. The economic dependence of the people on the reindeer determined the mobility of their lifestyle. Moving from place to place in search of seasonal pastures, the Nenets developed a sophisticated knowledge of their environment, which helped them to choose the best routes for wandering, handle the competition from other herders, and avoid a wide range of hazards, including diseases.

The way of life which the Nenets used to enjoy is known among anthropologists as nomadic pastoralism.

> Nomadic pastoralists are those who are primarily dependent on livestock, who live in environments with marked seasonality, and who choose as their basic strategy for providing year-round food for their herds the movement of livestock to pasturage rather than bringing of fodder to herds (Dyson-Hudson, 1980: 18).

The Nenets would have fitted quite well into the description of nomadic pastoralists as

> brave, independent, fierce men, freely moving their herds, ... having a pride, a hauteur, a strong sense of individual worth, and a strong sense of the nobility of pastoralism as a calling (Dyson-Hudson, 1980: 15).

The nomadic Nenets were organized into small isolated groups. Nomads could handle 'only a limited number of intensive face-to-face relationships and successfully distinguish among them' (Dyson-Hudson, 1980: 26-7). Such social and spatial organization was caused by the need of the people to adapt to the specific features of the natural environment, which 'set an approximate upper limit to the size of face-to-face communities'.

> In any given nomadically adapted population, efficiency of herding requires maintaining a herd of optimum size and structure, which in turn requires that the local subsistence groupings or camps of the

> nomads must also be maintained with an optimum range of size and structure (Dyson-Hudson, 1980: 26-7).

It seems reasonable to assume that the fractionalized social space of the small Nenets communities had an effect on their learning process, as well as on the people's perception of themselves. Looking specifically at song performance practice, it is important to recognize that every isolated small community created its own unique environment which allowed the emergence of many independent variations of the conventional model of song. Since Nenets nomadic society consisted of a large number of such small social units, each with its own melodic patterns, the proliferation of different melodic ideas within Nenets society as a whole became possible and even inevitable.

Erkar (clan). Kinship is more important to the Nenets than any other social relationship. There exist legends describing the origin of the *erkar* names, important symbols of the people's identity (Tereshchenko, 1960: 106-15). The significance of kinship is evident in the Nenets' song stories where the *erkar* of the epic hero is always described in great detail. When a hero meets someone, he is always asked: '*Erkarar namge?*' (What clan are you from?), and to a great extent the development of the plot depends on the hero's answer to this question.

In Nenets society, *erkar* is based on the lineage of the male members of the family. If a family becomes a target of someone's hostility or revenge, the boys must be saved and hidden first, since their existence is crucial for *erkar* survival. If a family man dies, the family extinguishes the fire in its *choom*'s hearth, a symbol of *erkar* continuity.

The Nenets word for family is *miad'ter*, which literally means 'filling a *choom*'. As the term signifies, throughout most of the Arctic year the Nenets leading a nomadic lifestyle used to be confined within the limited space of a *choom* filled with family members. Outside the *choom*, they were surrounded only by their livestock and silent tundra. Loneliness and separation from a larger community, as well as the necessity to withstand life's problems by themselves, was the price which Nenets families had to pay in order to cooperate with nature and maintain their economy.

Under such conditions, the environment in which the melodic patterns of the songs were established, then imitated and improvised upon, was traditionally limited to one family. Despite the narrow space of this learning environment, melodic creativity in these small communities seemed to be very dynamic. It is still typical for every Nenets family member to have quite diverse melodic repertory. The Nenets family is usually a source of many melodic patterns, and the explanation of this phenomenon can be found in the affiliation of a family member with a wider group of relations than simply those they share a home with: as a rule, a Nenets family consists of representatives of different clans. It seems illuminating that the principles of diversity and continuous re-creation characterize both the melodic creativity of the Nenets family members and the system of exogamous marriage, the rules of which the Nenets strictly follow.

Let us look more closely at the possible connections between the institution of exogamy and the dynamics of melodic creativity still typical for Nenets society.

Exogamy. James Frazer described exogamy as 'an unconscious mimicry of science', as a social law discovered by people through experience and intuition in their struggle for survival. He wrote:

> What they abhorred was really evil;
> what they preferred was really good ...
> the end which it accomplished was wise (Frazer, [1910] 1968 IV: 169).

Exogamy introduced a legal sanction against incest which was considered a crime that could damage offspring and so endanger the future of the whole community. This pre-scientific intuition was proven to have been well-founded: in the struggle for existence communities which did not follow the law of exogamy 'disappeared, having been either extinguished or absorbed by their more vigorous and prolific rivals' (Frazer, 1968 IV: 169).

The exploits of a hero who goes on a long and distant journey in order to win a wife from a clan of strangers is one of the major themes of the Nenets' songs. The theme is indicative of the significance of the exogamous institution in the Nenets' life, a fact also proven by the studies of ethnographers (Verbov, 1939; Dolgikh, 1970a). The epic stories explore the dillemma facing every mature Nenets man: 'whom may I marry?' The principles of exogamous intermarriages meant that the Nenets clans which migrated within the European part of the Nenets tundra continuously mixed with the far eastern group of clans. Such regulation of genetic heredity helped the development of the nomadic people into a healthy nation. But how did exogamy affect the development of Nenets cultural traditions?

This is almost an impossible question to answer, but it is noticeable that a similarity exists between the biological crossbreeding process based on the principle of diversity, and the musical creative process, also based on the principle of diversity. The similarity suggests the following hypothesis.

As a consequence of the exogamous marriages between men and women from distant clans, at least two different melodic patterns were usually brought together into one family, forming a rich resource for further melodic re-creations. The influx of various musical ideas was planted in a uniform stylistic ground which led to the development of an extremely diversified yet solid and enduring nationwide song tradition.

Exogamy also resulted in members of a clan becoming dispersed across a wide geographical area.

> [A] clan does not reside in the same locality, but has representatives in several different places. However, this lack of geographical basis does not cause its unity to be the less keenly felt (Durkheim, [1915]; 1965: 123).

> [T]he members of a single totem [or clan] are necessarily dispersed in different localities according to the chances of their marriages. As a result a totemic group [or clan] lacks a territorial base (Durkheim, 1965: 126).

Like the clan members themselves, the melodies created by the Nenets clans and families lacked a geographical identity, because they were also dispersed in different localities according to the chances of exogamous marriage. It is typical for the song traditions of agrarian sedentary peoples to have melodic styles associated with particular geographical locations. Nenets melodies became most associated with their performers' last names indicating the *erkar* and family origins of the performers. Perhaps, the last names of the Nenets performers can lead us to the roots of the stylistic similarities between the melodies, and may enable us to make a typological classification of Nenets melodies. If it is true that one melodic type can be associated with a clan name, then the whole diversified stock of the melodic types circulating within the song tradition can be perceived as a kind of genealogical tree.

Following this we can infer that performers with similar melodies in their repertories may belong to the same clan, and may even have the same names. Because it is typical for the Nenets to mark every song with an individual rhythmic idea, it seems likely that the similarities between the melodies can be identified in their melodic contour rather than their rhythmic configurations.

The three melodies recorded from Tikhon Apitsin illustrate just such a 'kinship' between the melodies. While rhythmic design is unique to each song, the modal aspect of the melodic intonations point to a pattern, which is just one among his many other melody patterns. If the same melodic pattern is found in the repertories of other performers with the name

Apitsin, it would give us a reason to consider the pattern representative of the clan tradition (see examples 3.20-3.22).

Of course, there can be found many other sets of melodies marked by affinities between themselves, such as the following two melodies, one recorded from Nataliia Taleieva in Nel'min Nos and another found in the Väisänen collection.

4.1a N. Taleieva, Nel'min Nos

4.1b Väisänen, 1965: 13

The pattern underlying the two melodies might have come from the same family environment, or belonged to the members of the same clan. Unfortunately, the data on the performer's last name is lacking in the Väisänen's publication, and we cannot, therefore, verify this connection.

The association of melodic types with family traditions is implicit, rather than explicit, in the musical sound itself. Parental features are not necessarily clearly noticeable in the appearance of their children. Likewise, the typological relations between the melodies are not necessarily audible, although they do exist between the melodies originating from one and the same melodic pattern.

The hypothesis that Nenets melodic types have an association with the last names of performers, and therefore, that melodic typology may parallel kinship typology, is not without foundation. The validity of the idea can be confirmed by an analogous correlation registered among the Southern Samoyed, the Teleuts and Shors, with respect to the drawings on shamanic drums. As Leonid Potapov suggested, the variations of the 'bura pictures' on the drums symbolized the identities of different clans: 'each clan deity rode a horse *bura* of a specific colour'. Therefore, he claimed the *bura* pictures were 'sources for establishing the clan composition of the Teleuts and Shors' (Potapov, 1978: 171). With regard to the Nenets, it is the melodic typology of the songs which seems to be the source for establishing the people's clan composition.

Song and a personal identity. Structured by society, Nenets song in turn serves as a structure for interaction and communication within society.[2] One of the social functions of Nenets song is that of personal identification. Performed in front of audiences, the melodic symbols combining collective and individual stylistic features reinforce the compound clan-family-personal identity of the singers.

The Nenets concept of 'personal' song has a complex connotation. It means that a person owns a magical song-name which protects him/her in ordinary life and represents him in the world of the supernatural. Among the Nenets, a person receives a song as a gift at each transitional stage of life: at birth, at the age of maturity, and at marriage (Pushkariova, 1990a). The social meaning of this custom becomes more explicit if we separate the notion of individual from the notion of person: a person, as opposed to an individual, must have a social status (Radcliffe-Brown, 1973: 308-9). In Nenets culture, it is a song melody which makes an individual a person. With ageing the social status of a person changes, and so does his/her song melody.

The Nenets' musical system of personal identification is similar to other systems of self-nomination discussed and analysed by Geertz.

> People everywhere have developed symbolic structures in terms of which persons are perceived not baldly as such, as mere unadorned members of the human race, but as representatives of certain distinct categories of persons, specific sorts of individuals (Geertz, 1966: 6).

While the native concept of personal song tells us that Nenets are aware of the nominative function of their melodies and of the social significance of their musical names, their custom of maintaining it as a symbolic system confirms Geertz's argument that the systems of nomination 'are not given in the nature of things – they are historically constructed, socially maintained, and individually applied' (Geertz, 1973: 6). The Nenets' personal songs fit perfectly into Geertz's theory on the orders of person-definition, especially into that part of the theory which discusses 'personal names' (Geertz, 1966: 13-22).

The 'personal musical stamps' of Sirionó in Bolivia were called by Nettl 'strange facts uncovered by musical ethnography and analysis' (Nettl, 1983: 9).[3] As for the Nenets' tradition of personal song, it has its own 'strangeness'. For a Nenets singer to claim a social and individual identity by performing a song, an original rhythmic idea has to be discovered. Other melodic parameters, such as scale, range, or melodic contour, often change in the process of performance, or they can be found in the songs of other singers, but the discovered rhythm of the song is unique. It remains stable throughout the entire performance, and becomes the signature by which that song will be recognized in future.

The extraordinary rhythmic inventiveness of the Nenets people is somewhat enigmatic, which makes us to look for some models of rhythmic sound and behaviour available in the performing context of the songs. Possibly, the sound of the shamanic drum played its role in the development of this stylistic feature. The intricate designs and drawings on shamanic drums often have a background of various kinds of grids. The regular beat of the shamanic drum probably acted as a measured grid-like background over which the Nenets could paint their intricate melodies.

However, today the Nenets soundscape lacks both the beating of the drum, and other musical practices based on rhythm. Maria Zhornitskaia, who has researched the dances of the northern people of Eurasia, could not detect a single example of dancing among the Nenets during her many years of the field research (Zhornitskaia, 1983). I did not see any physical activity stimulating the song rhythm during my song recording sessions either. I could associate the rhythmic nature of Nenets songs only with bird songs. It is, indeed, strange to discover that both types of songs are characterized by an amazing abundance of rhythmic designs, that they both fulfil the functions of identifying communities and individuals in these communities; and that like a Nenets singer, 'each individual bird interprets his song in his own way' (Brand, 1934: 32-4).

Musical rhythm appears to be the most inventive and variable aspect of the Nenets' musical system. To see if there are some spiritual motivations behind this creative impulse let us now look at the religious beliefs of the people.

Shamanistic beliefs as a key to the meaning of Nenets melody

The Nenets use their songs to serve many other goals than just story-telling. Musical expression is an essential part of the people's religious universe, a sacred language which they use to communicate with the world of supernatural. The native belief that music is sacred can be understood only in the context of the Nenets' religious ideology.

If one of the functions of religion is to frame a search for knowledge, shamanism fulfils this function in a unique way. Searching for knowledge in shamanism means an intensification of one's mental and emotional faculties during altered states of consciousness. Many scholars have attempted to identify how states of ecstasy and trance have yielded religious knowledge to shamans.

> [T]he ego may turn inwards to find a meaning in the surrounding world, when no meaning can be found in the external sensory stimulations (Nordland, 1963: 172).

Based on his studies of Tungus shamanism, Sergei Shirokogoroff defines shamanic ecstasy as a 'special favorable condition of the thinking process', or a 'perfection of means of cognition' (Shirokogoroff, 1935: 362, 376). Naming the shaman 'the one who knows', or 'the one who sees', the Tungus underline the cognitive goal of ecstatic experiences. This combination of 'knowing' and 'seeing' refers to the knowledge imported by visual images or hallucinations, a typical experience during altered states of consciousness which is perceived as real and valid.

Peoples in shamanistic cultures interpret the images of ecstatic experiences in accordance with their belief system. In turn, the hallucinations experienced during states of ecstasy tend to relate to these beliefs, and reinforce them as true and tangible.

Drumming and singing skills played a significant role in the ecstatic rites of shamans. It was quite natural for shamans to use music when communicating with the spirits. Thinking of music as a sacred language, they linked religion, ecstasy, and music together. Musical knowledge was, therefore, equated with religious knowledge.

According to Galina Grachiova, the Samoyed believe that melody is a person's *korsa* (thought), 'something created by the human brain'. They think of melody as a product of the innermost part, *kunsyzy* (the inside) of an individual, which, like a name, represents the individual in both the real and the supernatural world (Grachiova, 1984).

Each performer owns a number of such personal musical thoughts, which belong to him just as his body, dress, or name does. The melodies are believed to communicate their own meaning in addition to that of accompanying lyrics. When a shaman calls a spirit during a ritual, he may drop all the words of the song and let the melody 'speak' for itself (Grachiova, 1984: 195, 196).

The Samoyed associate themselves so closely with their melodies that they are concerned to protect their ownership of them. Singing other people's melodies is synonymous with stealing another's thoughts. As a form of theft, it is deserving of punishment (Grachiova, 1984: 195).

The Nenets believe that songs represent people in the world of the supernatural, and that spirits and gods recognize each person by his/her song. The animation of song is an integral part of their religious interpretation of the world based on the worship of spirits.

The animation of song

The belief that spirits reside in all parts of nature, for which Sir Edward Tylor coined the term 'animism', is innate to shamanistic culture. Because of its association with the evolutionist theory, this term has acquired a negative connotation among anthropologists. But the concept of animism remains appealing today to those scientific directions and ideological movements which view culture as the continuation of nature, and consider the boundaries between non-living and living matters to be blurred.[4]

The use of the traditional animistic concept by modern ecological movements, protesting against environmental abuse and advocating the inseparable unity of humans with nature, highlights the apparent universality of the moral and educational values of traditional animistic beliefs.

The Nenets' animistic beliefs are part of such universal values. Being an integral part of the traditional world-view of the people, they are used to serve many practical and educational goals, helping to maintain a healthy ecology and economy. The myths about the spirits residing in the surrounding tundra were used by Nenets adults to teach their children how to protect the environment and save it for future generations (Susoi, 1986: 114-15).

Identifying themselves with nature, the Samoyed created a pantheon of spiritual images. They sought to incorporate the spirits of nature into their lives, trying to influence them by magic and ritual. The hierarchy of the spirits in the Samoyed animistic complex included the Deer as life giver, the Sun as heaven's eye, Fire as *erkar*, and many other spirits highly honoured by the people (Vasil'iev, 1978). Until quite recently, the Nenets have treated Water as a living being, which explains why they used to have special melodies for lakes.

Song is also included in the Nenets' animistic complex. The animated Song is a traditional feature of Samoyed narratives. It plays the role of the third-person narrator, endorsed by the performer to lead and guide the story. As a character, Song finds heroes, introduces them to the listeners, gives them names, judges or sympathizes with them while watching and following them through their adventures. The Nenets call the animated Song character *vada-siudbabts* (word-song), or simply *siudbabts.* The Enets and Nganasan call it *meneko* (narrative) (Dolgikh, 1961: 5; 1976: 14-15). The character of Song is usually very active in the stories. It can fly and perform many other feats dictated by the plot. At the end of the stories, Song concludes that she is quite satisfied with what has happened, finally announcing: 'enough for the moment'.

The character of Song may also appear in the *iarabts* type of song. A typical plot is for Song to notice someone while it is sitting over a perch. It follows them and helps them through their adventures. Song is the subject in most of the formulaic expressions connecting and concluding epic episodes. It may say, for example: 'This time I have nothing to say, since nothing is happening for a while' (Kupriianova, 1965: 38-9).

The meaning of Song has different nuances. On the one hand, it is perceived as an abstract category, one of the living things in the world. On the other hand, as the Nenets concept of 'personal song' indicates, Song is always *a* Song, an individual thought of a concrete performer, who is the owner of that thought. Since the ownership of Song is usually due to its melody rather than poetic text (Pushkariova, 1990a: 82), the voice of the owner-performer is essential for the melody. The inseparability of a person's voice, thought and melody, so indisputable among the Nenets, makes us look for a reason for this in other concepts of the shamanistic culture.

Song melody as a totem

The term 'totem', or 'totemism', comes from the Ojibwa language of northern American Indians, who have an expression, *ototeman*, meaning 'he is a relative of mine' (Levi-Strauss, 1963: 18). The concept refers to the system of nomination based on the association of a clan and the clan's every member with a guardian spirit, who may be an animal, plant, or some other phenomenon of nature, and with whom the clan members share their name.

Like animism, the concept of totemism carries the 'stigma' of the time when it served 'to strengthen the case of those who tried to separate primitive institutions from our own' (Levi-Strauss, 1963: 103). Since then, however, the awareness of the similarities and differences between preliterate and written cultures has increased. The complexity of preliterate cultures has become apparent and more appreciated, and the 'definite parallelism of function' in the two types of cultures has been well recognized. I intend to revive here the concept of totemism as an instrument to understanding the Nenets concept of personal song.

Unlike the totemism of Australian aborigins or North American Indians, the Nenets do not appear to have had a consistent clan nomination system. Only some insignificant isolated features of totemism have been found among the Nenets, such as, for example, the tradition of naming the characters of song after reindeer.

It is perhaps surprising, therefore, to see the features of totemism in the custom of personal song, so widespread and still popular among Samoyed and other people of northern Eurasia. I am going to show how this custom fits into the 'old-fashioned' theory of totemism.

Scholars have always emphasized the multifarious interconnection of totemism with other social and cultural phenomena. They have indicated the coalescence of the following three elements essential to totemism:

> (1) a social element: the kinship of an animal or vegetable species, or an inanimate object, or perhaps a class of inanimate objects with an exogamous group or clan; (2) a psychological element: a belief in the kinship between members of the group and the animal, plant, or thing, often expressed in the idea that the human group is descended from it; (3) a ritual element: a respect for the animal, plant, or thing, typically manifested in a prohibition on eating the animal or plant, or on using the object, except on certain conditions (Rivers, 1941, II: 75, qouted from Levi-Strauss, 1963: 8).

It is significant that Levi-Strauss's definition does not limit totemic names merely to animals and plants, but also mentions other 'things', or 'objects'. Not only does Nenets personal song fit into the category of 'thing', but it also satisfies the social, psychological and ritual criteria of totem.

My proposed notion of song-totem would also fit within the all-inclusive schema of totemism developed by Levi-Strauss. He singles out a category of totemic phenomenon which identifies the relationship between particular totem and concrete person, and which absolutely matches the totemic function of personal melody (Levi-Strauss, 1963: 17).

Other existing definitions of totemism also allow us to include Song in the realm of totemic phenomena. According to James Frazer, totemism is

> an intimate relation which is supposed to exist between a group of kindred people on the one side and a species of natural or *artificial objects* on the other side, which objects are called the totems of the human group (Frazer, 1968 IV: 3-4).

Frazer distinguishes totem from fetish, or amulet, because:

> totem is never an isolated individual, but always *a class of material objects*, generally a species of animals or of plants, more rarely ... *a class of artificial objects* (Frazer, 1968 IV: 4).

Obviously, scholars have never limited totem to animals and plants. In addition to natural totems, like clouds, rain, hail, the moon, the sun, water, sea, they have presupposed all kinds of 'artificial objects' being used as totems. Frazer illustrates the category of artificial objects by such things as 'net, tent, knife'. If we extend the category of 'artificial objects' to other things produced by human thought and creativity, song would fit into that category.

The definition of totemism proposed by Durkheim allows for the inclusion of song into the totemic system of nomination as well. Durkheim argues against a limited understanding of totemism and assumes the possibility of its various manifestations.

> [If] we reduce totemism to a sort of animal or plant worship, we have seen its most superficial aspect: we have even misunderstood its real nature (Durkheim, 1965: 109).

He defines totem broadly as a name, or emblem, which satisfies the social need of 'representing the idea ... by means of material and external signs, *no matter what these signs may be*' (Durkheim, 1965: 149). The following description of totem is fully applicable to the custom of personal song among the Nenets.

> [T]otem ... has appeared to us as something relatively outside of the man, for it is only upon external things that we have seen it represented. *They* [people] *do not put their totems upon the things they possess but they put it upon their persons, it becomes a part of them,* and this world of representation is even by far the more important one (Durkheim, 1965: 136).

The Nenets' song-totem is characterized by its individual character, which relegates it to the category of individual totems also mentioned by Frazer and Levi-Strauss. A person establishes the ties of mutual respect and protection with an individual totem. It 'begins and ends with the individual man, and is not like a clan totem transmitted by inheritance' (Frazer, 1968 I: 49). There are various ways of acquiring an individual totem, and one of the ways described is exactly parallel to the Nenets custom of acquiring personal song.

> Sometimes the individual totem is not acquired by the individual himself ..., but is *fixed for him independently of his will at birth* (Frazer, 1968 I: 59).

While Frazer illustrates this custom with the drawings which are made on the floor before a child is born and later used as the child's individual totems, the Nenets are accustomed to sing a song to a newborn child, which later becomes the child's personal song.

Frazer fully realized that totemism was not a fixed model in the minds of the people, but one subject to flux.

> The social system sometimes survives the religious; and, on the other hand, religion sometimes bears traces of totemism in countries where the social system based on totemism has disappeared (Frazer, 1968 I: 4).

We can now see an illustration to Frazer's insight: in the case of the development of Nenets totemism, all the religious and social conditions which shaped their beliefs have disappeared except for some traces left in the musical practice of the people.

The Nenets custom of personal song is a representation of totemism in the contemporary world, which allows us to appreciate the people who, being faithful to their thoughts and beliefs, have preserved for us the unique and most valuable musical artifacts of a socio-ideological system which no longer exists.

Shamanism[5]

The numerous definitions of shaman, the central figure of the magico-religious complex, mention a wide range of shaman's roles and activities: shaman is a religious specialist, who performs the roles of a priest, a prophet, a magician, and a medicine man. Each of the functions by itself can describe the shaman neither fully nor exactly. It is most important that the

Plate 1 Indiga

Plate 2 S. Apitsin and his companion, M. Argeieva, Indiga

Plate 3 Grandchildren of Ie. Belugina, Indiga

Plate 4 Indiga

Plate 5 F. Belugin, Indiga

Plate 6 Ie. Belugina, Indiga

shaman – a charismatic personality, elaborating on the traditional mythological knowledge and the established order of things, healing and curing people – gains his status through mastering personal and direct communication with the supernatural world through ecstasy. The 'archaic techniques of ecstasy' (Eliade, 1964) define the very meaning of shamanism, in which the role of shaman is primarily that of a mediator between a group of people and the world of the supernatural. Taking a path inward, into an ordinarily 'hidden reality' of the altered state of consciousness, requires technical expertise. The shaman, called the 'master of spirits', is supposed to have the extraordinary capacity to attain and utilize the state of ecstasy for various social purposes.

The process of attaining ecstasy is described as a journey, the ascent of the shaman's spirit to heaven, which brings him into direct contact with celestial powers. This journey is essential to the form of shamanism observed in the indigenous cultures of Central Asia, Siberia, and the Arctic regions of Eurasia. During a theoretical discussion held in September 1981 at the Sarospatak (Hungary) symposium 'Shamanism in Eurasia', the term shamanism was approved as a concept embracing all early forms of religion, including 'spirit possession' and 'mediumship'. The scholars decided not to 'be afraid to call shamans shamans', and to use the culture-specific term (originated from the Siberian Tungus [Evenki]-Mongol language) as a standard umbrella-category for the variety of related phenomena (Lewis, 1984: 3-13).

Nenets shamanism[6]

Open shamanistic practices among the Arctic peoples disappeared under the Soviet regime, which attacked shamans and religion in general. The European Nenets were the first Arctic nation which stopped conducting public shamanistic ceremonies. From both the practical and ideological points of view, research on shamanism became a complicated issue for Soviet ethnographers, who had to rely upon information about shamanism contained in the writings of travellers, missionaries and scholars of the 18th and 19th centuries (Khomich, 1966: 209-17).

The tradition of teaching and learning the skills of shamans developed its rules, symbols, and customs. At a male child's birth, the family would look for a special sign, such as a mole, or other unusual feature. In adolescence, when a boy became too nervous, the people thought he was possessed by torturing spirits. As a rule, gifted and talented individuals, unusually sensitive and extraordinarily creative, became the candidates for the shamanic profession. Quite often such individuals were born into the families of professional shamans.

If an adolescent boy showed the signs of 'madness' (a tendency to sleep and to sing a lot), he was ready for the initiation to the profession. After his initiation he could start his training under the supervision of an elderly experienced shaman. Shamanic education was a long process with several stages and lasting many years (Khomich, 1978).

The early stages of shaman initiation quickly provided the student with some of the simple methods of ritual behaviour. Long after this initial schooling, the teacher continued to control and direct the student shaman. Even once he was allowed to participate in shamanic ritual, a student shaman (*mal tadebe*) was not supposed to have a drum. Only after seven years could he start looking for an appropriate tree from which he could make his drum and drum stick. The beginner's drum, however, could not have the hanging pendants which distinguished those of established shamans. After a further ten years, the status of the student-shaman changed. He received recognition as a professional, and became *yaumpoi,* or *inutana.* The complete process of education lasted about twenty years.

There were different specializations within the profession, or different degrees of power which shamans possessed to control the spirits (Hajdu, 1968: 165). The most powerful shamans *(vydutana)* went on spiritual journeys to heal people. They had all the ritual attributes necessary for communication with the spirits, such as the costume, the drum, and the staff (pole) – the sacred tool and the symbol of their authority. There were also 'medium' shamans *(ya'niany),* who performed easier duties, such as healing those with minor ailments, and 'small' shamans *(sambana)*, who were responsible only for burial ceremonies.

The ritual ceremony performed by the shamans in front of local audiences was called *tadebtenos'* in Nenets and *kamlanie* in Russian. The Russian term is a derivative from the Turkish word *kam*, meaning shaman (Kenin-Lopsan, 1987: 21). According to the available descriptions of the Nenets' shamanic ritual made by 19th-century observers, the ritual usually took place inside the *chooms*. The Nenets would invite shamans to their homes when they became sick and needed help. The ritual could last for a number of hours during either the day or night. It was a spectacle in which the shaman dressed up in his costume and behaved like an actor interacting with the invisible characters of the drama taking place in his imagination.

The spectacle would normally begin with the shaman warming up his drum over a fire, and with an introductory beating on the drum. Gradually, he would accelerate the drum beat, adding to it vocal calls and exclamations. From time to time, the shaman would stop beating the drum in order to describe to the audience his conversation with the spirits. At any given time, he might burst out singing a song describing his travel to the upper world. By the end of the ritual, he had completely abandoned reality, and had immersed himself into a trance. Once he had woken up and his consciousness had returned to this world, the shaman would announce his judgment about the sick person, telling the family whether their relative was likely to die or to survive. During his seance, the shaman was often helped by an assistant, one of his young students, whose task was to imitate the shaman's actions and echo his words and melodies (Khomich, 1966: 215-16).

The democratized rite of ecstasy

Shamanism as a professional institution no longer exists in the Arctic region, and the theatrical attributes of the shamanic ritual are kept today in museum collections. However, scholars believe that it is premature to speak of its complete disappearance, since there are many people who still 'retain elements of shamanism'. Taksami talks about these people as just 'ordinary citizens taking part in daily production and public affairs', who occasionally enter an ecstatic state 'for their own sake' (Taksami, 1984: 455-6). That relates to an observation, made earlier by Shirokogoroff, that every Tungus is able to shamanize and experience the communication with the spirits (Shirokogoroff, 1935: 376), and to some facts, submitted by Khomich, that in the past, 'everybody could shamanize among the Nenets', that initially, Nenets shamans did not take a fee (*haso*) for their service, and that financial inequality between the shamans and the rest of the community developed only by the beginning of the 20th century (Khomich, 1966: 209, 216-17). It seems understandable that as emerging professionals shamans drew upon a communal experience of the ecstatic rite, which used to be an integral part of the traditional culture.

The custom of the 'democratized', 'general inspirational', or 'family shamanism' typical of many Arctic peoples, has already been discussed earlier in this book (see p. 41) with respect to the sharing of the same artistic knowledge by shamans and the people. Obviously, they shared not only the artistic tradition, but the technique of ecstatic rite as well. Due to their early evinced talents and mental predispositions to ecstatic experiences, shamans were chosen to lead a community of people on such ecstatic journeys, and conduct negotiations with the spirits on the people's behalf in ritual settings. But in some individual cases, the shaman was 'not necessarily a better psychologist than his common kinsmen', which has led scholars to see the difference between the ecstatic technique of professional shamans and common visionaries as being a matter of degree which depends on the individuals themselves (Hultkrantz, 1978: 34; 1984: 31, 55).

Many respected fieldworkers have reported that people in shamanic communities can experience ecstatic inspiration during musical performances. Castren mentions an epic singer whose posture and behavioural features reminded him of shamans (Castren, 1860: 343, 457). Shirokogoroff portrays a singer who is not a professional shaman, but who shamanizes and hallucinates during his performance. He describes how a performance which began monotonously, 'gradually becomes passionate and ... culminates in a scream of ecstasy when spirits enter the shaman' (Shirokogoroff, 1935: 327). Donner writes about some Samoyed performers who 'compose and sing as if they are under the influence of drink' (Donner, 1926: 1). Hatto remarks on some epic improvisations characterized by a 'dream- or trance-like style', and an 'excitement bordering on ecstasy' (Hatto, 1970). In a later study, he writes that sometimes, when the epic singers narrate in the first person, they seem to be 'possessed by a hero or other divinities' (Hatto, 1981: 14).

These observations suggest that the ecstatic journeys, which singers quite often experience as they sing, are the source of the variety of symbols filling the plots of native mythology, including the journey-ascent into the supernatural world, which appears to be a verbalized image of the people's journey-transition into the inner layers of their consciousness.

The emotional ascents are imagined as climbing on a tree, pillar, or mountain; flying into the sky, or heavens; or swimming in a river. Consistent with the image of ascent, a vertical stripe on a shaman's drum symbolizes a 'ladder'. Various vehicles – spirits, birds, horses, reindeer, or fishes – escort the people into the inner/upper world (Hultkrantz, 1978: 38). In Samoyed mythology, Song is also portrayed as a means of ascent. It is one of the vehicles 'upon which the singer betakes himself into the supernatural world' (Emsheimer, 1991b: 162). Melody is a thought, *korsu*, of a singer, but it is also a rope, umbilical cord, string, or a thread ascending to the heavens, symbolizing the singer's life but ceasing to exist when he/she dies.

Scholars have been intrigued by the ability of performers experiencing the altered state of consciousness to exercise control over the structure and meaning of their performances.

> Does he [the shaman] perform his duties in a trance, or is he conscious of his actions throughout the ceremony? (Cushing, 1981: 226).

Observing that drumming and singing usually took place during the initial phase of ecstatic rite, fieldworkers have tended to associate the musical performances with a 'more shallow waking trance' (Hultkrantz, 1978: 43).

In order to explain the apparent contradiction between the unconscious state of trance and conscious music making, ethnologists have turned to psychologists for ideas. As a result of looking into the data of psychology it has been discovered that during altered states of consciousness the level of creativity actually increases, which explains why folklore performances taking place under these special psychological conditions sometimes produce extraordinary results (Banyai, 1984).

One of the most detailed studies on the altered states of consciousness, by Ronald Fischer, confirms this conclusion. It reveals that it is just on the threshold of ecstasy[7] that the highest concentration of thought, the sharpening of all the senses, and the rising of all creative capacities occur. A cartography of the inner space suggested by Fischer shows the position of ecstasy among the other altered states of consciousness. The circle-like map depicts the transcendental experience as a voyage from 'I' to 'Self', in which 'I' is the point of departure, normal daily routine thinking, while 'Self' is the Oneness, the realm of unity where there is no form, no name, no concept.

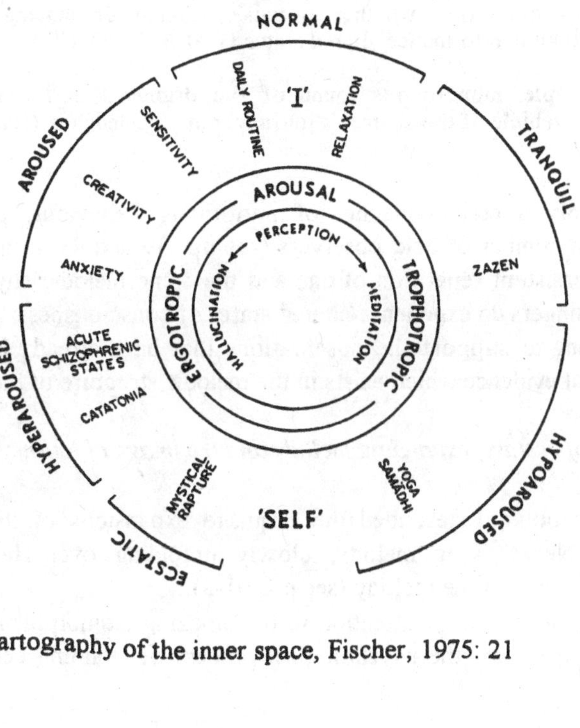

4.2 A cartography of the inner space, Fischer, 1975: 21

This chart serves as a classificatory model of the states, which helps us to associate the states with different cultural traditions. The left wing of the whole circle outlines the *ergotropic* type of arousal typical for the ecstatic practices in shamanistic culture, whereas the right wing of the circle outlines an alternative way to the 'Self', based on the *trophotropic* type of arousal experienced in Yoga meditations. The final state of the process – ecstasy – results from a creative breakthrough out of catatonic hyperarousal. It manifests the absolute certainty which is interpreted in accordance with some mythology or belief system.

In the light of this information, the high quality of song performances during the pursuit of ecstasy seems normal and natural. On the Fischer's map, the psychological state of such performances can be associated with the *creativity* phase of the aroused states.

There are special features pertinent to song which make it the appropriate vehicle for the ecstatic journey. Melodic repetition and rhythm are the two elements of musical performance which are most recognized as stimulating ecstasy, especially among Siberian shamans.

> [E]ntrainment in both shamanism and yoga is facilitated by concentration on repetitive driving stimuli (Doore, 1988: 222).
>
> Rhythmic stimulation, whether by music, singing, or dancing, has long been known to induce altered states (Walsh, 1990: 173).
>
> [T]he simple, monotonous sound of the drumbeat is the most common vehicle of the shaman's journey, not psychedelics (Harner, 1988: 12).

Thus, not only a certain manner of performing behaviour, previously described by a number of field observers (see pp. 39 and 43-4: notes 3 and 4), but the persistent repetition of one and the same melodic rhythm may indicate that singers do experience altered states of consciousness while they sing. I am going to support the observations that have already been made with additional evidence which exists in the melodic structure of the songs.

The oneness of ecstasy, expanding melody and the image of journey-ascent

Earlier in this book, I described the exquisite expansions of the interval structure of Nenets song melody, slowly unfolding over rhythmically identical repetitions of the melody (see pp. 61-3).

I would like now to draw attention to the amazing isomorphism between the melodic expansion, the psychological process of attaining ecstasy, and the people's interpretation of the world.

Musical concepts do not 'speak' in the literary sense, but they contain and deliver a meaning which may have a parallel interpretation in the linguistic mode of expression. The verbal concept of shamanic journey-ascent is one of the most conspicuous parallelisms of this kind. It puts into words the emotional and intellectual journey which singers are able to structure musically. The ascending melodic lines of the Nenets' songs almost literally lay the pathways to the sky. Indeed, such melodies communicate the same semantic meaning as the words (Grachiova, 1984: 200).

Moreover, both the ascending melody and the verbal concept of journey-ascent reflect the psychological condition of the singers, who experience during song performances a gradual heightening of emotion which ultimately alters the state of their consciousness.

According to psychologists, the transcendental experience is channelled into the three parallel processes: emotional, motor, and cognitive functions. A heightened emotional state inevitably affects the motor and cognitive functions. With regard to motor behaviour, psychologists have registered a significant 'reduction of exteroceptive stimulation and/or motor activity' during the altered states (Ludwig, 1969: 10). Usually, a gradual turning inward toward the mental dimensions takes place at the expense of the physical movement: 'there is neither capacity nor necessity for motor verification of the intense sensations' (Fischer, 1975: 10, 15).

In contrast to the features of motor behaviour, the cognitive process becomes positively affected by the increase of emotional tension: the creative capacity of thought significantly increases in parallel with emotional arousal. Such a 'cooperation' of emotion and thought results in a sharpening of creative abilities. In neurological terms, the creative state is described as the coupling of subcortical arousal with a cortical (cognitive) interpretation of that arousal. 'The experience is symbolic', say psychologists. It is immediately transformed into a visual image, a melody, or a taste (Fischer, 1975: 2). The unity of the aroused emotion with the cognitive process is conducive to the evolution of novel relations, the 'changes in the formal characteristics of thought', and new meanings.

> An aroused creative state ... can be characterized by an increase in both content (a description of space) and rate of data processing (more intense time) (Fischer, 1975: 10).

Let us apply this psychological theory to the unity of ecstasy, expanding melody, and the shamanic image of journey ascent, distinguishing some of the Nenets' song performances. We can see how the theory and the practice verify each other by answering the question of how the three channels of the transcendental experiences – emotional, motor, and cognitive – manifest themselves in the song performances.

(1) The gradual emotional ascent is quite apparent in various aspects of the performances, such as the agitated voice of the performer, the increased volume and accelerating tempo, and the expanding range of the reiterated melody.

(2) The motor behaviour of the performers at these moments shows exactly the same pattern as psychologists find in the behaviour of those who pursue and experience the ecstatic state. As a rule, the performers look completely detached from reality. Even at the moment of musical culmination, the singers sit motionless, not paying much attention to the audience. In psychological terms, these moments demonstrate 'an inward shift in the direction of attention', and a 'drastic reduction of motor activity' and 'sensory input'.

(3) The structural consistency and sophistication of the melodic expansions perfectly illustrates the cooperation of emotion and thought, which results in the sharpening of creative abilities during the psychological transitions. Showing the 'changes in the formal characteristics of thought' in regard to musical space and time, the expansions bring into the performances a new elevating meaning, a meta-meaning uncovering the realm of shamanic spirituality. As every expanding melody reveals the 'advent' of a person's spiritual journey-ascent into his/her inner space, the meaning of the song transcends beyond the content of unfolding verbal narrative into the space of the fundamental cultural images.

Thus, the Nenets' expanding melodies testify to the validity of the quoted psychological theories, as well as providing a new case important for further developments of these theories.

The parallelism of verbal, musical and psychological structures is also a perfect illustration of Peirce's theory of iconicity. In Peirce's definition, an icon is 'a sign which stands for something merely because it resembles it'. An icon is a sign 'partaking in the characters of the object', whose 'qualities resemble those of that object, and excite analogous sensations in the mind for which it is a likeness' (Peirce, 1931-35, vol. 3: 362; vol 4: 531; vol 2: 299). In the Nenets' melodic expansions, musical sound partakes in the 'likeness' which embraces an array of cultural symbols and metaphors. The phenomenon of Nenets expanding melodies is a beautiful example of musical iconicity.

The similarity between the structural qualities of musical sound and the meanings of linguistic concepts was initially addressed by Erich von Hornbostel (1927: 83-9), and then by Alan Merriam (1964: 85-101).

Merriam associated 'the interrelationships among all the senses', 'perceptual matching', 'associated sensation', or 'intersense transfer' with the phenomenon of synesthesia, which occurs when a stimulation in one sense area finds an equivalent representation in another one. Outlining the scope of issues related to the subject, Merriam pointed out their importance to the field of ethnomusicology:

> The problems of synesthesia and intersense modalities fall under the general rubric of concepts which underlie a music system, and the highly involved questions they raise lead to consideration of further problems of music and language, aesthetics, and the interrelationship among the arts (Merriam, 1964: 85).

Illustrating synesthesia, Merriam emphasized its well-known manifestation in the intersensual perception of colour and musical sound, happening when 'the subject hears music and at the same time sees colours'. However, he was well aware of the existence of other intersense transfers. He regretted the paucity of cross-cultural evidence on the subject of synesthesia (1964: 96), which he thought could explain the origin of matching structures in a fundamental concept underlying a whole culture.

We face an example of such cultural syncretism in the Nenets' song tradition. The fundamental concept underlying Nenets traditional culture is the concept of *ascent* to the supernatural world. As the concept touches upon different sensual and symbolic dimensions of the people's minds and creativity, including the structural aspect of song melodies, it reveals to us the intriguing phenomenon of synesthesia.

Psychologists define synesthesia as a phenomenon of 'joined sensation', 'sensory blending' which is 'frequently projected outside the individual, rather than being an image in the mind's eye' (Cytowic, 1989, 1995). They point out that synesthesia may occur during altered states of consciousness as a result of the regression of thought away from the dominance of the cortical level of consciousness towards the overwhelming emotion driven by the subcortical level of consciousness. The integration of interpretive cognitive (cortical) and interpreted emotional (subcortical) structures characteristic of the ecstatic hypoaroused state makes possible the syncretic experiences, which are characterized by a fusion of senses, an easy transformation of meaning from one symbol to another, and a resulting uniformity of the symbolic structures (Deikman, 1969: 31; Pahnke and Richards, 1969: 408; Ludwig, 1969: 15; Fischer, 1975: 32). The isomorphism of psychological and musical structures and its interpretation in the shamanic mythology by the concept of journey-ascent supports the observations of these scientists.

The Nenets' expanding melodies provide a confirmation and reinforcement of those ethnomusicological studies which discuss a similar phenomenon observed in the songs of the Yakut (a Turkish-speaking people who live east of the northern Samoyed). In the mid-1950s, Grigory Grigorian described the phenomenon of 'unfolding mode' he found in Yakut songs (Grigor'ian, 1956: 72, 75; 1957: 342-3). Some twenty years later, Eduard Alekseiev, the author of a more detailed study on the Yakut songs, suggested that the same melodic phenomenon ought to be present in other song traditions, most probably in the musical performances of a 'high emotional intensity' (Alekseiev, 1973; 1976: 57). Nenets melodic expansions indicate that Alekseev was correct. Moreover, revealing the intimate relations between song and shamanistic culture, they suggest the possibility that the unity of musical, verbal, and religious expressions will sooner or later be discovered in the song traditions of other shamanistic people in the Arctic and Siberia.

Nenets expanding melodies, therefore, provide confirmation of many theories and hypotheses offered by philosophers, scientists, and musical scholars. More importantly, they confirm and reinforce the concepts and beliefs of the people themselves.

The circularity of the relationship between belief and experience raised the question about the roles of the two in this relationship.

> [T]o what extent do spiritual practitioners *create* their tradition's cosmology from their experience and to what extent is their experience *created by*, or at least molded by, their cosmology? To what extent do religious practice and experience create beliefs and to what extent do beliefs create religious experience? Which is chicken and which is egg, or are they mutually interdependent? (Walsh, 1990: 115-16).

Assessing the interdependence of ecstatic experiences and cosmological worldview, Walsh emphasizes the significance of the ideological factor which in his opinion outweighs the natural causes. When a person enters the state of shamanic ecstasy, the mind is prepared for what follows in accordance with a belief system which makes sense of the ecstatic experience. Relying on the established conventions of various systems of symbolic expression, society cultivates, supports, and guides the interpretation of the ecstatic rites (Walsh, 1990: 173). The unity of the psychological, musical and ideological factors characterizing the described performances of Nenets song exemplifies such an interplay of nature, culture, and society.

A microcosm of a vanishing shamanistic culture, and a sign of the ecstatic rite, Nenets song releases to us important information which might shed some light on the most challenging area of musical science – the study of musical thought and cognition.

Notes

1. Nettl, 1994: 141.
2. Correspondence between societal and musical systems is also inherent in song communication among birds. As Peter Marler points out, the structural patterns of bird song 'serve the particular societal structure of the species' (Marler, 1977: 49-50).
3. The phenomenon of the personal ownership of songs is discussed by Nettl in relation to the song tradition of the Blackfoot Indians (Nettl, 1989: 140-43).
4. Some recent scholarly publications contain revivalistic statements which sound reminiscent of the 'earth-based' spiritualities of shamanistic people:

   > [T]he art is sacred ... not only are humans and nonhuman nature part of the interconnected web of life, but also ... spirits reside in matter, as well as in other dimensions (Orenstein, 1993: 172).

5. The earliest bibliography of the Russian literature on shamanism included more than 650 titles (Popov, 1932). A later bibliography on only Siberian shamanism consisted of almost 1000 titles (Swienko, 1984). There were archives on Siberian shamanism in the Museum of Anthropology and Ethnography named after Peter the First in St Petersburg, and in Budapest (Voigt, 1978: 59).
6. Samoyed peoples have similar words for shaman: *tadebe* in Nenets, *ta(a)debe* in Enets, *tetepe* in Sel'kup, *ta(a)rabe* in Kamas, *tade(e)* in Mator. The root of all these terms can be found in the Nenets word *tadera* which means 'to be excited', or 'to be mad'.
7. Discussing the relation between music and the altered states of consciousness at book length, Gilbert Rouget insists on music inherence in trance rather than in ecstasy. He argues: 'ecstasy never makes use of it [music] at all, there is an inherent incompatibility between the practice of ecstasy and music' (Rouget, 1980: 11-12). The author's position is based on his view of trance and ecstasy as two different transitory states. This view is, however, in contradition with the theory of the altered states of consciousness (Tart, 1969: 1-8); Ludwig, 1969: 9), and the psychologists' use of the concept of trance interchangeably with the concept of altered states of consciousness (Houston, 1975: 59; Gill, 1978: 157). According to this theory, ecstasy is one among many other altered or transitory states, whereas trance is an umbrella category for all of them. The relation between trance and ecstasy is, thus, overlapping and hierarchical. Ecstasy is a state of trance, which often, contrary to Rouget's characteristic, is the culmination point of musical creativity and inspiration.

CHAPTER FIVE

Some Thoughts about Song Melody

> When one shouts, he is not thinking;
> When he sings, he is thinking![1]
>
> It is not emotion that organizes expression, ...
> It is expression that organizes emotion.[2]

The folk notion of melody as thought and its scientific counterparts

The current preoccupation with cognitive scientific approaches and the rising interest in musical cognition falls in line with various traditions of thought that have explored these territories before. Although it is usually the ancient Greeks who are credited with the earliest inquiries into the mind (Gardner, 1985), some of the roots of cognitive science can be also identified with similarly insightful experiences and ideas in eastern civilizations and preliterate cultures.

The Samoyed people's concept that music is a thought originating in the brain runs along this line. This insight is probably due to the introspective orientation of the shamanistic minds experienced in exploring the 'inner space'. The introvert psychology of shamanistic cultures led Shirokogoroff to define one of them as a 'psychomental complex', consisting of the two levels of conceptualization: 'immediate reactions' to the world which are of 'a permanent and definite character', and a 'complex of ideas' which define these reactions and which may be 'regarded as a theoretical system' (Shirokogoroff, 1935: 1).

Such a differentiation, based on the cultural phenomena observed among the Tungus, parallels similar classification by the theorists of intelligence, who indicate the two main kinds of cognition – ordinary cognition and metacognition. Ordinary cognition is what is actually known, whereas metacognition 'refers to knowledge about', or 'the awareness of what one does or does not know' (Sternberg, 1986: 4-5). Neuropsychologists outline this difference in other terms: thought emerging in the brain as a direct and immediate response to reality is a product of 'instrumental' consciousness, whereas analytical thought which reflects on other thoughts is characteristic of 'intentional' or 'self-referential' consciousness, 'a domain of socially and culturally determined verbal discourse' (Pribram, 1978: 577, 579). 'Musical thinking' and 'thinking about music' singled out by Nettl as separate categories (Nettl, 1994) can be associated with instrumental and self-referential consciousness respectively.

So far, however, the scientific concept of musical thought is no more than a blanket term referring to mental processes which have not yet been fully identified and comprehended.[3] It is still based, partially, on intuition, lacking a theory which would elaborate on the musical aspects of 'the modularity of mind' (Fodor, 1983). Nevertheless, the idea that music is a thought is paving its way towards the definition of music.

As Nettl points out, the difficulties in defining 'music' are overwhelming and confusing (Nettl, 1983: 15-19; 1989: 46-9). Music occupies a unique but indiscrete place among other modes of thought in the mind and culture. It inherently requires overt physical behaviour in order to be produced, multiplies into various vocal and instrumental versions, and ramifies into notation, print, and recordings. It is also reflected in the endless interpretations of those who listen to and think about music. As a form of nonverbal communication comparable with the sound communication of animals, first of all, songbirds, it is also indiscrete on the phylogenetic continuum.

Can a focusing on the cognitive nature of music help musical analysts and philosophers to account for such a variegated complexity? Not if the cognitive criterion enters the definition of music in a dictatorial manner, as if it is the last and uncontestable truth, destined to dismiss and replace all previously existing definitions of music.[4] This has already been recognized in scientific research: 'Science commits suicide when she adopts a creed' (Julian Huxley, quoted by Berg, 1969).

Since the progress of 'increasing awareness' depends on the accumulation of knowledge which reflects various aspects of a phenomenon, only an all-inclusive mosaic of vigorous ideas can represent that large number of elements which coexist, correlate, intertwine, and overlap within every single whole.

A comprehensive definition of music is an ongoing and selective process moving in the directions of numerous disciplines.[5] As for the cognitive approach, more than any other approach it presupposes infringements on the territories of psychology, linguistics, semiotics, biology, and cognitive science. So far, the involvement of musical disciplines with this interdisciplinary direction differs in degree.

Anthropologically oriented ethnomusicologists, who focus mainly on musical behaviour, 'have not really paid much attention to the concept of musical thinking as an activity distinct from other kinds of thought, or to the notion of music as residing in a particular portion of the brain' (Nettl, 1994: 139). Ethnomusicologists who have come from a music background, on the other hand, do tend to consider traditional music in terms of intelligence. They think of traditional music as a symbolic production 'which, like language for a given community, is transmitted from mouth to ear, from generation to generation, and represents a major constituent of the group's cultural identity' (Aaron, 1994: 137). Musical intelligence, they propose, needs to be studied from the point of view of (1) an organism's adaptation to its environment, (2) the mental structures required for such adaptation, and (3) the ability of an individual to learn and use these structures according to the circumstances. The focus in such studies should be on the structural complexity of musical systems and the consistency of the systems with their socio-cultural contexts (Aaron, 1994: 138).

The discipline of music theory, dealing by definition with formal musical systems (though predominantly with the formal systems of Western art music) adopted the cognitive approaches to musical research with more ease and earlier than ethnomusicologists. Its merging with psychology has provided a foundation of musical knowledge for the modern field of music psychology (Butler, 1992). Based on this tradition, a multidisciplinary field of 'music cognition' has recently arisen, in which 'music theorists and psychologists', have been 'joined by scholars in philosophy, linguistics, and artificial intelligence' (Jones and Holleran, 1992).

In the field of music education, great respect and popularity has been gained by the theory of multiple intelligences which considers musical intelligence on a par with linguistic and other forms of intelligence (Gardner, 1983). Music educators have adopted this theory with excitement, finding it an excellent means of promoting and propagating the role and value of music education in our society, and of supporting the arguments against intelligence tests which focus only on linguistic and mathematical skills (Brummet, 1997).

Thus, the cognitive approach to music is taking different routes to penetrate and influence how we think about music. But it originates in and spreads from the mainstream of cognitive science defined as the study of intelligence and intelligence systems (Simon and Kaplan, 1989: 2).[6] The field has been formed out of three main channels of intellectual development: (1) structural studies of symbolic communication systems; (2) similar explorations of neurophysiological and biological systems which underlie the symbolic systems; and (3) studies of artificial intelligence aiming to create computer models for both types of systems. According to a relatively recent account of cognitive science, its principal contributing disciplines have been psychology, artificial intelligence, linguistics, philosophy, and neuroscience.

The discipline of music is not mentioned as being among other contributing fields, including social psychology and cognitive anthropology (Posner, 1989: 2-7).

The necessity to explore music as a unique mode of thought and cognition is implicit in the recently revived idea of consilience, or the unity of knowledge (Wilson, 1998).[7] Expressing the holistic image of the world, in which different phenomena are governed by the same fundamental laws, the idea has repeatedly emerged in the philosophies of different civilizations. A major contribution to the consilience of knowledge and, therefore, the consilience of academic disciplines, has been Peirce's semiotics, which provides a philosophical ground for understanding music in terms of thought and cognition.

Is song melody an icon, index, or symbol?

Semiotics interprets the world as a web of interrelated signs.[8] To the semiotician, everything can be read as a sign relating to something else. The relationships of things to one another are in constant flux, progressing without limitation in space and in time. The whole of the phenomenal reality is a single dynamic process, which, depending on the school of thought, has been called evolution or semiosis.[9] For an evolutionist, human culture is a 'psycho-social phase' of the 'unitary process of evolution' (Huxley, 1956). For a semiotician, human culture is 'anthroposemiosis', the specific extention of 'biosemiosis' (including 'zoo-' and 'phytosemiosis') which is in turn the extension of 'physiosemiosis'.[10]

Semiosis and the model of intelligence

Cultural semiosis is based on the relationship between the mind and the collective total of all that is presented to the mind regardless of its correspondence to real life. Signs are vehicles which convey something to the mind from outside, and also represent the mind to the outside. Thus, the whole of life experience becomes an interpretation which is mediated and sustained by signs.

This interpretation is both fluid and regenerative, because every sign when it symbolizes an object, does so to some extent inadequately. The inadequacies lead to variation and accumulation of change. Therefore, sign-symbols do not just exist, but continuously develop and multiply.

> A symbol, once in being, spreads among the peoples. In use and in experience its meaning grows (Peirce, 1931, vol. 2: 300-302).

Dynamics and change, growth and infinity represent only one side of the thinking process. The other half constitutes continuity and generality, stability and coherence, which glue the endless renewal and regeneration of thought into a consistent web.

> Every thought must address some other, ...
> all which is reflected upon has a past (Peirce, 1931, vol 5: 253).

Studies of the brain give more concrete contours to Peirce's abstract picture of semiosis. They highlight that the dual character of intelligence reflected in the combination of dynamism and stability of symbolic systems is caused by the inner- and outer-oriented work of the brain.

> Brain structure is influenced by cultural events which in turn become structured by brains. ... Information processes are akin to those described by the second law of thermodynamics, which deals with the organization of energy rather than its transference and conservation (Pribram, 1978: 578).

Like computer hardware and software, brain and culture cannot work without each other. Their mutual collaboration is capable of both preserving and reproducing information which is partly deducible from already existing information and partly unpredictable. Not only language, but every mode of symbolic communication is due to the mechanism of intelligence based on the brain/culture correlation. Such an understanding dismisses the linguocentric perception that intelligence manifests itself only through language. It also explains why the basic theoretical dichotomies known as 'linguistic models' can be applicable to other systems of communication, including those of animal communication.

The most serious claim on the territory of intelligence made by animals is bird song. It is through the interplay between brain, society and culture that intelligence manifests itself in bird song, uncovering the intelligent nature of music in general (Snowdon, Ch. and Hausberger, M., 1997; Abramovich-Gomon, 1998).

The use of Peirce's sign categories for the problem of meaning

Of the three vectors of symbolic systems' comparisons – meaning, structure, and function – the comparisons along the vector of meaning have been the most difficult ones to handle. This is despite the fact that psychologists take meaning for granted, and consider it innate to individual expression independent of symbolic material.

> [A] human being is a biological system living in a biological environment. When thinking man is considered strictly together with his environment, the problem of meaning largely dissolves. ...[T]here is no psychological problem of meaning *per se* (Humphrey, 1963: viii).

As much as meaning is inherent in the relation of the individual to the environment, it is also inseparable from the structure of expression, whether it is structuralized sound, visual material, or physical movement. The inseparability of expression and meaning applies to music as well. There is no such thing as musical sound 'by itself' without a meaning: the two are one and the same thing.

This is consistent with the view of semioticians, for whom any act of structuralization (including, of course, a structuralization by means of musical sound) is essentially meaningful.

> It is impossible to draw an absolute boundary between [structural] body and meaning in the realm of culture. ...
>
> In art meaning is totally inseparable from all the details of the material body incarnating it. ...
>
> A work of art is meaningful all the way through (Bakhtin [Medvedev], 1928: 22; quoted from Ivanov, 1974: 311).

But it is just the 'specific peculiarities' or 'qualitative distinctiveness' of symbol which determine its special meaning and usage in culture and society. Every symbolic modality conveys a unique meaning and fulfils a unique ideological function irreplaceable by those of other symbolic modalities (Bakhtin [Medvedev], 1928: 11; quoted from Ivanov, 1974: 313).

The uniqueness of music has been discussed mostly in its relation to language, partly because of the rigour of the linguistic theory which has inspired the comparison and naturally because the two modes share the auditory-oral track of processing information and sound as symbolic material structuring the information. It is not surprising, therefore, that studies aiming at comparing language and music have proliferated over the last 30 years (Nettl, 1983: 23). Over and over again, scholars have pondered the question of the uniqueness of music compared to language (Levman, 1992; Kraut, 1992; Raffman, 1992; 1993).

The semiotic point of view provides a common ground for the comparisons between music and language. The analysis of the signification process and the elaborate typology of the functions of signs accomplished by Peirce offer a key to understanding the ways in which music functions as a mode of signification.

Peirce divides the process of thought formation into the three instances which he names 'firstness', 'secondness', and 'thirdness', and which seem to be the equivalents of the psychological functions of 'sensation', 'perception', and 'cognition'.[11]

'Thirdness', or cognition, is crucial to the completion of a mental sign. It crowns sensation and perception with the production of thought and the development of knowledge based on learning and memory. Cognition is a form of semiosis. Without cognition there is no communication, no sign which is in Peirce's words 'something by knowing which we know something more' (Hardwick, 1977: 31-32).

Peirce also shows how the meaning of sign depends on its various relations to the object it signifies. He introduces three basic types of such relations: (1) iconic relation, which emerges at the level of sensation, and results in a structural similarity between sign and its object; (2) indexical relation, which emerges at the level of perception, and establishes a referential connection between sign and its object; and (3) symbolic relation, which emerges at the level of cognition under the laws of the logical system to which the sign submits itself in order to be understood (Peirce, 1931, vol. 2: 275, 449).

Thus, according to Peirce, a mental sign becomes a symbol when it functions as an element of a logically organized system of communication designed in accordance with a collective convention. But as it becomes adjusted to the system, the sign preserves its iconical and indexical relations to the signified object which have been shaped at the levels of sensation and perception. The essence of symbol is its *polyfunctionality*.

Depending on the modality and certain psycho-social conditions of the signification process, one of the three functions of the symbol may be fulfilled more than the others. It becomes a matter of degree whether sign acts more like an icon, index, or symbol. Such a flexibility of symbolic signification is conditioned by a culture, mode, style, genre and other constraints of expression. Not only do the dynamics of signification reflect a complex relationship between the symbol and the signified object, but it also reveals how uniquely an individual expression in a particular symbolic system and in a particular culture signifies and communicates meaning.

Peirce's classification of signs into icons, indexes and symbols sometimes produces a delusion that there are three separate categories of signs rather than three functions of signification co-existing in one sign. Although scholars have emphasized the combination of the three different functions in signs,[12] there has been a tendency to explain the difference between language and music by associating the former with symbol and the latter mainly with icon and index.

> [T]he musical sign is basically an icon or an index. ... Symbols in the sense of Peirce, conventional signs, are only marginally important in music (Nöth, 1990: 432-3).

Such underestimation of the symbolic qualities of musical sign misrepresents both music as a means of communication and the logic of Peirce's theory. Conventional rules are a prerequisite for communications and cognition in all symbolic modalities. There hardly exists any systematic thought and communication without them. Nöth's conjecture that symbolic function is insignificant for music automatically reduces the role of musical sign in the realm of cognition, and implies that music has little to do with intelligence, conventional norms, arbitrariness, organized thinking, learning, and knowledge. If musical sign is not a symbol, it is then an incomplete sign incapable of serving as a means of communication. Note that Peirce avoids privileging the symbolic character of verbal signs at the expense of non-verbal signs. On the contrary, his model of semiosis is all-inclusive, capable of embracing various symbolic modalities.

The negative attitude towards the symbolic qualities of musical sign originates not only in linguocentrism, but also in the over-exaggeration of the role of emotion in music at the expense of the role of thought. Thought organizes emotion by imposing a symbolic structure on sensation and perception.

> [I]t is not emotion that organizes expression but, on the contrary, it is expression that organizes emotion (Bakhtin [Voloshinov], 1929: 101; Ivanov, 1974: 327).

What makes musical expression meaningful is the transformation of emotional experiences into a coherent sound structure based on conventional rules. It is important in this regard to point out that neuropsychologists clearly distinguish between emotional processes in the brain and those which underly expression (Pribram, 1978: 574).

Iconicity and indexicality, indeed, are important features of musical sign, but they are entwined into symbolic systems which are arbitrary to a certain extent.[13] If there were no arbitrariness in symbolic expression, we would not have such a diversity of languages, as well as musical styles and traditions in world cultures. This diversity is due to the arbitrariness lying 'at the heart of all symbols, giving them their power of application to nature and reality', and requiring that a community of minds 'will meet in mutual, mirroring consciousness' (Trevarthen, 1990: 690).

The fact that musical diversity exceeds language diversity (there are more musical traditions and styles in the world than there are languages) makes the study of music especially rewarding for ethnologists interested in the diversity of human intellectual achievements (Khalfa, 1994: 10). An examination of Nenets musical culture offers many such rewards. Let us summarize the findings as they seem to be relevant illustrations to the on-going theoretical discussion.

The folk notion that music is a thought appears to be an intuitive parallel to the modern scientific concept of music cognition.

Like cognitive scientists, the Nenets favour the introspective rather than the behavioural approach to understanding music. They are aware of the inner impulses, which regulate a person's character, mood, and behaviour, and show this awareness in various speech idioms and customs.[14] In accordance with their attitude towards music, the people associate melodies with the functioning of the brain.

In common with semioticians, the Nenets realize the uniqueness of the material and structural qualities of the musical symbol, and assign to music a special ideological function irreplaceable by other signs. Viewing and valuing individual musical thoughts as material products, they apply to them the law of personal intellectual ownership.

The melodic system of Nenets song shows all the characteristics of a symbolic system revealing the psycho-social nature of intelligence. Reflecting the dual mechanism of intelligence working as the brain/culture correlation, the musical tradition of the Nenets constitutes a dynamic yet stereotypical system conditioned by culture, society, and individuals. It shows, however, a unique proportion between the collective and individual, the conventional and innovative features within the system, and it implements iconic and indexical functions of musical symbol in a peculiar way determined by the traditional society, culture and religious ideology.

The inner polyfunctionality of musical sign provides Nenets melodies with different layers of meaning which have been revealed through a series of contextual analyses (chapter 4). In terms of the symbolic function, the structural design of the Nenets' musical system reflects the essential aspects of traditional society: nomadism, clan organization, and exogamy. In terms of the indexical function, the music refers to the identities of individuals, and groups of individuals, as well as that of the entire nation. In terms of the iconic function, the music 'photographs' the immediate sensations of individuals who undertake the journey into the depths of their consciousness. Every single Nenets melody is a microcosm of all the enlisted functions and qualities of musical thought, and every single Nenets melody is a testimony to the validity of the people's ideas about music.

The idea that melody *is* a mode of thought has passed the test of time. At first, a sparkle of intuition, it has become a scientific paradigm intriguing by its unexplored dimensions and potential discoveries.

The paradigm status of melody in song

We have seen in the foregoing chapters how important music was to shamanistic cultures. Within the hierarchy of their values, it had the status of a sacred language, superior to normal everyday speech. Within the hierarchy of semiotic systems, the status of music is also special by the extent of its mysteriousness. A great part of the unsolved mystery is the problem of musical meaning.

The universe of musical meaning

Most attempts to understand the uniqueness of musical meaning have so far been made from linguistic perspectives with the result that sometimes music is deprived of any meaning at all.

> Music presents ... the problem of a semiotic system *without a semantic level (or a content plane)* (Eco, 1979: 11).

The implication of the discussion which has taken place in this book is that there is no doubt as to whether there is musical meaning, but there is a question about the nature of this meaning.

Even scholars of music cognition who do recognize music as a system of communication put the verb 'communicate' in quotation marks when applying it to music. They continue to ask what it is that music actually 'communicates':

> Is there a semantics of music, and can it be compared to well established semantic systems for natural language? (Jones and Holleran, 1992: 4)

Alternatively, they discuss the problem of the ineffability of musical knowledge, a conscious knowledge that cannot be communicated in words: 'Does music mean what it cannot say?' (Raffman, 1993: 37). Admitting that the analogy between music and natural language is 'irresistible', they make various proposals for a system of musical semantics, and utilize linguistic categories for this purpose. For example, the quality of 'indeterminacy' of meaning in language has been extrapolated on meaning in music, and a point has been made that musical meaning is, like language, both 'indeterminate' and 'determinate' (Kraut, 1992).[15] This conclusion, however, does not reveal any more than Peirce's concept of semiosis has already revealed. It is clear from the concept, and Peirce's philosophy in general, that both indeterminacy and determinacy of meaning are inevitable for any symbol, act of communication, culture, or semiosis. Semiosis is a never-ending potential of meanings, a 'series of successive interpretants' *ad infinitum* (Peirce, 1931, vol. 2: 92, 303).

Thus, on a comparative scale, the problem of meaning becomes a matter of degree from the point of view of basically two problems: to what extent meaning is indeterminate and ineffable in a mode which, like language, has a dictionary, and to what extent meaning is determinate and effable in a mode which, like music, does not have a dictionary.

Even without having an exact instrument that can measure the space of the semantic fields of language and music, we can say that the content plane of language is vast, but the content plane of music is vaster. If the meaning of music is a universe, then language is a planet within this universe.

The apparent overlap of the two semantic spaces is easy to comprehend by looking at a concrete form, determined by culture, mode, style, genre, individual mind, behaviour, and concrete situation. Song is one such form. The various culture-specific meanings of the form's hypostasies in Nenets song has been already discussed. Now, let us think about the meaning of song in general.

The primacy of melody

Song is a ubiquitous and timeless musical form, the origin of which goes back to animal and even insect communications.[16]

> Song began on earth in insects and amphibians, but reached its peak of development (in land animals other than man) in birds, who alone of the large groups have adequate sense organs, brains, and habits to make them even remote competitors with man as musicians (Hartshorne, 1973: 34).

A broad definition of song as 'a vocalization ... that is repeated in more or less continuous, regular patterns' (Smith, 1977: 563), true for both bird and human song, highlights the principle of melodic repetition as the fundamental idea of song which cuts across different species and cultures of all ages. Like the foundation of our mind, melodic repetition exists 'in psychological eternity in which there is no past, no present, and no future' (Hall and Nordby, 1978: 121; Freud, 1933: 104-5).

A diversified knowledge about an essential component of song – melody – comes from different disciplines. Musical psychologists define melody as a form of both behaviour and cognition. Musical theorists identify four basic features of melody: contour (the pattern of rises and falls), interval size, key or tonality (the pattern of tonal relationships), and rhythm. Folklorists identify the traces of melody in language and call it 'prosody' and 'metrics'. They also recognize the essential role of melody in song.

> Melody is the original impulse, which captures all aspects of aesthetic speech, and gives to the shapeless material a structural harmony and grace (Zhirmunsky, 1975: 439).

The primacy of melody in song is noticeable not only from the structural point of view. It is also observable in the act of performance. As soon as a performer 'opens his mouth to sing', Albert Lord writes, he 'begins establishing the primary element of the form – the rhythm and the melody' (Lord, 1960).

James Porter reports a similar phenomenon. Interviewing a Scottish ballad singer, he asks her: 'which is more important, the tune of a song or the text of a song?' And the singer assures the scholar that her air comes first:

> I think if you get the air o' a sang, the words are nae ill to learn. The words ... would come second. That's my opinion. And once you get the air in yer heid, then ye can easily learn the words (Porter, 1976: 20-21).

The same pattern of memory activation characterizes Nenets singers. When they prepare to sing, they first take a few moments for silent concentration, in order to recover a musical idea from their inner being, then they 'release' the musical idea with a couple of meaningless syllables or exclamations, and only after that, do they begin attaching strings of words to the persistently reiterated melody.

Among the Lapps and the Karelians, there exist special genres of song, such as Lapp *juoiggam* or Karelian *joiku*, in which large portions of melody are just vocalizations of a single syllable (Stepanova and Koski, 1977). For many other Arctic peoples words in song are sometimes not even necessary. Waldermar Jochel'son writes about the Yukaghir people who 'start improvising, stringing senseless words together into a kind of sing-song, having afterwards not the slightest idea of the contents' (Jochel'son, 1926: 42-60; Christiansen, 1953: 43).

Having considered the structural and behavioural signs of the primacy and superiority of melody in song, how can we now signify its role in shaping the meaning of song? It is my contention that the concept grasping the hierarchical relationship between musical and verbal thought in song already exists. Perfectly defining the status of musical thought in song is the concept of 'paradigm'. Jakobson has applied the notion of paradigm to the traces of melody in poetry. But if the idea works for poetry, it is even more apt for song.

In its most general sense, the notion of paradigm is equivalent to the meaning of 'model' or 'pattern'. It embraces a complex hierarchy of models and patterns, which explains why the term 'paradigm' has been so overused. Echoing the popularity of Thomas Khun's 'scientific paradigm' (Kuhn, 1970), it has appeared in a countless number of library titles. Much earlier, though, the concept was implemented in the linguistic theory of Ferdinand Saussure, who was the first to define the syntagmatic and associative (paradigmatic) relationship constituting language.

> In a linguistic state ... everything depends on relations. How do they work? The relations and differences between linguistic items fall into two quite distinct kinds, each giving rise to a separate order of values. The opposition between these two orders brings out the specific character of each. They correspond to two different forms of mental activity, both indispensable to the working of a language (Saussure, 1986: 121).

Saussure defined the linear, or horizontal type of relationship between linguistic units as 'syntagmatic', and the complementary vertical type of relationship as 'associative', or, to match the first term, 'paradigmatic'.

> Outside the context of discourse, words having something in common are associated together in memory. In this way they form groups, the members of which may be related in various ways. ... This kind of connexion between words is of quite a different order. It is not based on linear sequence. It is a connexion in the brain. Such connexions are part of that accumulated store which is the form the language takes in an individual's brain. We shall call these 'associative relations' (Saussure, 1986: 121-2).

To match the term syntagmatic, the term associative was then replaced by the term paradigmatic. The paradigmatic type of relation between linguistic elements meant the 'relation of choice', a 'potentiality of occurrence and substitution of linguistic elements and even classes of words which occupy the same position within the same context'. Eventually, semioticians extended the syntagmatic and paradigmatic dimensions of language, applying them to other semiotic systems, and the thought process in general. Paradigm in this broadest sense became understood as a potentiality, a possibility for a substitution of adequate elements, and a choice of alternatives within a certain pattern. As such the concept was used by Jakobson in his theory of poetics.

Jakobson called the paradigmatic dimension of poetic structure a vertical 'axis of selection', and he characterized it by the principles of 'equivalence, similarity and dissimilarity, synonymity and antonymity', as opposed to the syntagmatic dimension, a horizontal 'axis of combination', which he called 'the build up of the sequence based on contiguity' (Jakobson, 1960: 358).

Jakobson indicated the difference between the paradigmatic relationships in colloquial language and in poetry. The phenomenon of paradigm in speech is a potential of linguistic alternatives which are not present in the discourse until they actually get selected. Available in dictionaries, they become audible only when used.

In contrast, the paradigmatic dimension in poetry is based on explicit rather than implicit equivalency. Repetition and parallelism, or a musical background of poetry, is superimposed on syntagmatic structures continuously open for word substitutions.

Jakobson specifically points out that the paradigmatic axis of relations between repetitious melody and linguistic structures in poetry, or 'the projection of the equational principle into syntagmatic dimension has a much deeper and wider significance' than just producing a phonological effect. It 'inevitably involves semantic equivalence,' responsible for the 'multiplex, polysemantic essence' of poetry (Jakobson, 1960: 368, 370).

It is clear that the 'multiplex, polysemantic essence' is also 'an inherent and effective property' of song, where it exists due to the same 'enduring thing' – continuously reified melodic message. Moreover, the message finds a more complete realization and fulfilment in song than it does in poetry. It is not a coincidence that most of Jakobson's illustrations of the paradigmatic dimension of poetry are folk song texts, which emerge during musical performances and have real melodies as opposed to implicit rather metaphorical melodies of poetry (Jakobson, 1960: 364, 369).

The melody-paradigm of song is the source for a limitless number of word substitutions. Words flowing in parallel to the melody-paradigm narrow it every time in a new way. The overall message is indeed ambiguous and multi-sided in the sense of the relation between the musical and verbal symbols, and in the sense of the relation of both symbols to experience.

> Icons are the accomplished image of an experience that is already past, while index is linked to an ongoing experience in the present. The symbol, however, always possesses a general meaning and is based on a general law; everything that is truly general is related to the indefinite future ... ; it is a potentiality whose mode is *esse in futuro* (Jakobson, 1983: 91-2).

The musical paradigm of song obeys the general laws of the musical system, just as words obey the general laws of grammar. The semantic potentiality of melody, however, exceeds the meaning of words. Words in song come and go, marking melody with particular meanings, while song melody endures with a promise to embrace an unlimited array of verbal meanings. Not only does the melodic paradigm of song allow for various word substitutions throughout a single performance, but it remains an open resource for more, and to some extent, unpredictable semantic interpretations, possible indefinitely.

The pre-verbal origin of musical thought within the pyramid of consciousness

As they mirror the ineffable brain processes, musical structures provide guidance in revealing these processes. A discovery of a correspondence between an element of a musical structure and a physical reaction in the brain may shed light on the way the musical mind works. More enlightening, however, are those extrapolations of the structural phenomena on the working of the brain which exercise a synthesis of structural and evolutionary approaches, taking into account the evolutionary histories of the brain and musical cognition. In such investigations, song and symphony, for example, would be associated not only with different paths and regions in the brain but also with different realms in the history of the musical mind. In anticipation of these scientific advancements, it seems interesting to preview the place of song in the realm of consciousness.

Some of the specialists in the field of psychology consider consciousness 'indefinable'.

> To ask 'What is consciousness?' does not appear to be unreasonable; yet the question does not seem to be fully answerable in reasonable terms. So, along with questions like 'What is God?' and 'What is life?' we generally rule out consciousness from scientific inquiry (Ornstein, 1972: ix).

But there are also those who accept the challenge, and take the risk of pinpointing the essence of the phenomenon. One such definition derives from the thought that 'the world we know is constructed':

> [C]onsciousness is structure, is form, and *is* the content (Fischer, 1975: 1).

Centred on the quality of structuralization, this definition seems to embrace every mental function which creates an order and imposes the order on the environment.

The evolutionary idea of the gradually unfolding consciousness gives consciousness the shape of a pyramid. The metaphor visualizes the stratification of consciousness, or the accumulation of structures which over the course of growth and development exchange positions of dominance with each other: there are long-term as well as temporary dominants in the pyramid.

> The dominants are similar to pyramids, the top is in the cortex of the left hemisphere, the body is in the cortex of the right hemisphere, and the foundation reaches the deepest structures of the brain (Traugott, 1978: 715).

The pyramid-metaphor shows that the essence of the evolution of consciousness is in the accumulation of different cognitive functions. Newly developed functions work in parallel with the previously emerged functions which have not been discharged and remain in operation. It reveals the complexity of all realms of consciousness: the foundation is as complex as the top, and the complexity of the top depends on the complexity of the foundation. The functional specialization of the pyramid's planes is based on the principle of cooperation and exchange. The consciousness utilizes the planes selectively, in accordance with different tasks.

Where does melody, the paradigm of song, reside within the pyramid? Although scientists have not yet been able to identify the musical planes of the pyramid of consciousness, some theories and observations sporadically generated by various studies may show the ways to answering this question in the future.

The pre-verbal features of musical thought

The 'right brain revolution' in cognitive studies has uncovered the specialization of the right side of the brain in non-verbal types of thought. A large part of this knowledge has come from the observations of brain-injured people. It has been noticed that patients after a surgical removal of Broca's (linguistic) area in the left part of their brain lose the ability to talk, while retaining some ability to think and remaining conscious intelligent personalities. On the other hand, those with injury to the right side of their brain lose basic musical functions, along with the ability to understand the emotional connotations of words and sentences, metaphors and proverbs. However, it has been also discovered that musical functions have a much wider distribution over the brain rather than being wholly localized in the right hemisphere. While 'average individuals have a right-hemisphere superiority in musical tasks', professional musicians show a left brain superiority in musical thinking (Gardner, 1975: 345). Musical functions have also been located in the most primitive lower parts of the brain, and in 'the subcortical structures important in rhythmic perception and emotional arousal' (Gardner, 1975: 348-9).

The observational data show the difference between those musical abilities and structures which constitute the condition of musical thinking antecedent to language, and those manifestations of musical thinking which develop in parallel with language. The findings support the scenario of music evolution as originated in the semiotic theory of non-verbal communication.

The theory highlights the 'component sub-systems of human communication that are found elsewhere in the animal kingdom as well'. It identifies the controversial position of music as a non-verbal systems of communication (Sebeok, 1972:163). On the one hand, according to evidence provided by bird-song research, it has traits continuous and shared with non-speaking animals. On the other hand, it has developed into sophisticated forms, which belong uniquely to human beings. A solution to the controversy has been made by a recognition of the pre-verbal origin of communication by means of repetitive melodic patterns which humans inherited from other animal species. Then, side by side with verbal communication, they developed more complex musical forms 'far exceeding anything that any other animal is known to produce' (Sebeok, 1977: 1060).

Bird-song research provides a strong evidence on the pre-verbal origin of musical rhythm and repetition essential to the melody of human song as well. Outside bird-song research, however, the evidence on the pre-verbal origin of musical rhythm has been, so far, unsystematic,[17] and even less attention has been paid to repetition as a property of pre-verbal musical thought.

Musicologists-aestheticians focusing only on Western art music 'propose to address seriously ... the function of repeats in absolute music' which they consider 'a problem in the philosophy of art' (Kivy, 1993: 329). They ask questions about repetition, having in mind the musical compositions of the 20th century characterized by a 'continuous mutation' of form.

> It may well be asked, does musical repetition have to be? Is it written in the book of nature that music must be based on the principle of repetition? And the answer clearly is *no*. For this is a normative as well as a descriptive principle, and the composer is free to observe it, or to rebel against it, as he or she sees fit (Kivy, 1993: 359).

The narrowness of considering musical repetition as just a means of composition in contemporary art music, as opposed to a universal phenomenon fundamental to the evolution of communication, blocks the way to discovering an answer to a remarkable question which has a much broader connotation:

> Our understanding of musical technique would have advanced much further if only someone had asked: Where, when, and how did music first develop its most striking and distinctive characteristic – repetition? (quoted from Kivy, 1993: 327).

Philologists, in turn, study repetition as a phenomenon of discourse, or a feature of poetry, rather than a musical phenomenon:

> Repetition is a very widespread phenomenon. Repetition is characteristic of poetry and prose literature, of adults' everyday talk and of children's talk and talk to children; it is a powerful persuasive strategy and an essential cohesive strategy (Johnstone, 1987: 210).

At the same time, they do not let it go unnoticed that repetition exists at the foundation of the brain's developmental process, that it is the first device of discourse learned by children and the last one to be lost in schizophrenia and aphasia (Johnstone, 1987: 207). When linguistic functions become reduced to a certain low level, a 'habit of repeating words', frequently and seemingly involuntarily, is all that is left of the ability to speak a language (Gardner, 1975: 11, 14, 53).

More support for the primary position of musical thought in the pyramid of consciousness is provided by theories on the expanding mind and altered states of consciousness. In different terms they describe a reverse of consciousness towards primary conditions, as opposed to the progressive unfolding of consciousness towards the top of the pyramid where more differentiated and detailed structures emerge. On the path to ecstasy consciousness turns backwards, it is 'infolding', 'regressing', liberating itself from logic and rational thought and concentrating on the holistic undifferentiated type of thought. In terms of the theory of deautomatization, what happens is 'the undoing of automatic perceptual and cognitive structures,' which 'permits a gain in sensory intensity and richness at the expense of abstract categorization and differentiation' (Deikman, 1969: 34).

During ecstatic regression, thought takes a musical direction. Moving towards intense emotion, concentration of meaning, abstract images and forms of expression, the meaning of thought loses detail, but gains on holistic vision. The forms constructed at the depth of the pyramid are usually elementary and unelaborated. They are 'form constants',[18] musical rhythms and ornaments, all pertinent to the synesthetic and hallucinatory experiences accompanying the regression.

> The tendency of ornamentalization is not reserved to visual imagery, but also governs the order of poetic and musical rhythm, imposing an all-pervasive metrum and harmony on the hallucinatory creative-religious states (Fischer, 1975: 32).

There is an assumption that musical rhythms are subjective, that they become a part of the 'psychophysical make-up of the individual', probably because they have ties 'with electric activity of the brain'. Since 'the frequency of the basic brain wave does vary from one individual to another' and 'remains more or less constant in a given individual throughout his life', a discovery of a personal rhythm may even be genetically determined (Siikala, 1978: 44).

Is there a cognitive value in musical rhythms? Can we call them the symbols of thought? And if so, then what kind of cognitive function do they fulfil?

Nenets song provides an answer to the questions. It brings a credibility to the compatible ideas selected and quoted above, while being itself explained through these ideas. Let us now gather the 'answers' together into one conception.

Nenets song is governed by melody, which is a manifestation of thought because it is a structure, an order imposed on a subjective emotional experience. It is a thought, because it constrains the emotion, and has enough power and plasticity to withstand even the excitement of pre-ecstatic states. It is a thought-symbol, because it fulfils the function of nomination. Each Nenets melody is like a personal name, reflecting the 'psychological make-up' of the individual and connecting with the electrical activity of that person's brain. Nenets melody illustrates that naming is indeed 'one of the chief methods for imposing order on perception' (Tyler, 1969: 6), and in so doing it dismisses the linguocentric argument that the act of nomination can be associated only with words (Maruszewski, 1975: 157).

The shaman's ecstatic rite is a journey within the pyramid of consciousness. During the journey, the Nenets reach the foundation of the pyramid, the original birth place of reiterated melodic message. Descending along the vertical dimension of the pyramid (and visualizing the process as ascendence instead) they experience the world of expanded consciousness represented by the image of a pyramid. The latter operates as a paradigm, because the hierarchy of the cognitive functions within the pyramid is in accordance with the principle of associative relations. Functioning as a paradigm unfolding in the course of evolution, the pyramid of consciousness has retained the ability to infold and reverse the course. Thus the accumulated resource of mental functions available within the pyramid of consciousness offers many opportunities to cultures and individuals who make choices: they utilize the refined multilevel structure of consciousness in various ways and for various reasons and purposes.

The Nenets are masters of the non-verbal mind. Being aware that words have their limitations, they feel comfortable within the state of consciousness where musical thought is powerful, valuable, and sacred.

Notes

1. Congo Basongye people (quoted from Merriam, 1964: 64).
2. Quoted from Bakhtin/Voloshinov, 1972: 101.
3. These mental processes have been described, for example, as 'brain energy arousal, appearing in large groups of discrete neurones at the level of several specified cortical areas, more or less transiently correlated' (Wallin, 1991: 19).
4. Here is an example of the exclusive treatment of the cogntive approach to music: 'I conclude that various implicit definitions of music, such as music-as-notation, music-as-emotion, and even music-as-sound are at best in need of repair; I propose the idea of music as cognition for their replacement' (Serafine, 1988: ix).
5. A draft of a future cross-disciplinary definition of music has been proposed by Wallin as a part of his outline of perspectives on biomusicology: 'Music is an open system of evolving structures growing into sounding artifacts which not only consume actual time but also generate virtual time; the system and its space-time structures are ultimately conditioned by bio-geocultural parameters of behaviour and deportment. Music is basically perceived unilaterally in the right cerebral hemispheres through the auditory system in a bilateral coordination with senso-motoric limbic and associative brain functions (the autonomous systems included) within a framework of multimodal experiences' (Wallin, 1991: 16).
6. In the mid-1980s, cognitive science was introduced as 'the mind's new science' formed by the mid-1970s (Gardner, 1985).
7. The dictionary meanings of 'consilience' is 'act of concurring; coincidence; concurrence'. 'The consilience of inductions takes place

when one class of facts coincides with an induction obtained from another different class' (*Webster's Revised Unabridged Dictionary*, 1913).

8. The analogy between sign relations and a spider's web belongs to J. von Uexkull (Deely, 1990, 14).
9. 'Semiosis' has been defined as 'sign process', signification process', or 'communication process' which is made possible by the organization of signification systems' (Sebeok, 1986: 887).
10. 'Anthroposemiosis' refers to the sign processes which are species-specifically human. 'Biosemiosis' defines the capacity of all living organisms to exchange information with their environment by means of signs. It includes 'zoosemiosis', the phenomenon of animal communication, and 'phytosemiosis', the sign interaction of plants with their environment. 'Physiosemiosis' refers to the physical interaction of things in so-called inorganic nature (Deely, 1990: 28-31).
11. 'Firstness' is a feeling, merely a potentiality lacking recognition or analysis, which is analogous to sensation defined by contemporary psychologists as a 'transformation of energy that impinges upon any of our sensory receptors (retina, cochlea, eye) into neural information' (Hodges, 1996: 134). 'Secondness' is a relation of feeling to something external based on the realization of external fact, which is analogous with the phenomenon of perception, defined as a utilization of 'sensory information to make further sense of the world' (Hodges, 1996: 134). 'Thirdness' is a synthesis of the two previous instants of experience with learning, memory, conventional rules, or saying all in one word – thought. It implies cognition defined as 'the acquisition, storage, retrieval, and use of knowledge obtained through the sensory and perceptual systems' (Hodges, 1996: 134).
12. Like any other sign quality, iconicity is 'a matter of degree arbitrarily and culturally coded' (Eco, 1976: 191). As linguists have recently discovered, language is 'more iconic that it is generally believed' (Waugh, 1992: 8). Following Sebeok's call 'to illuminate the psychological bases' of iconicity (Sebeok, 1976: 1434), conclusions have been made that 'iconicity is involved in the perception of all objects', that iconic signs existing only in consciousness are 'the nexus and origin of semiosis in the biological community' (Deely, 1986: 29).
13. Like iconicity, arbitrariness is a term specifying a relation between sign and object. Unlike iconicity, which means a quality of similarity between sign and object, arbitrariness means a quality of structural independence of sign from its object: 'it is purely arbitrary to join one idea to one sound rather than to another' (Peirce, 1931, vol. 1: 1).
14. For example, to be in a good mood in Nenets means 'the inside is solid', to get upset means 'the inside got worse' (Tereshchenko, 1990: 35). At the rites of consecration, the older shaman gives his cap to a successor 'as if transferring to him his brains' (Popov, 1944).
15. At the roots of this discussion is W. Quine's argument that the semantics of natural language is indeterminate to the extent that every utterance may have different yet equally correct interpretations (Quine, 1960). Departing from this similarity between language and music, Kraut argues that musical semantics also has determinate features which are defined by the genre of the musical piece and 'its intended audience'.

16. The evidence of song undermines L. Meyer's thought that there are no musical universals. Ignoring this rather conspicuous musical universal would threaten to obscure the role of musical thought in the origin of intelligence. The fact that ethnomusicologists have been studying song more extensively than any other musical specialists undermines another of Meyer's arguments – that ethnomusicologists do not pay attention to musical universals (Meyer, 1998: 5-6). Indeed, ethnomusicologists tend to be suspicious of generalizations, but only if they are based exclusively on the examples of Western art music. It is the continuous exploration of world music cultures by ethnomusicologists that has led to discoveries of the musical universals integral to the evolution of culture and intelligence.
17. According to neurologist Hans Ustvedt, a loss of language causes a 'regression to a more infantile approach to music, with the most primitive elements (rhythm) better preserved than those of moderate complexity (melody)' (quoted from Gardner, 1975: 340).
18. Term used by Cytowic, 1995: 8.

Conclusion

Nenets song has been interpreted in this book as a microcosm that enfolds the whole of the traditional shamanistic culture, and as a stronghold of that culture in the present life of the people. As the retrospective contextual analyses of the song's melodic system have shown, musical performances have played an exclusive role in 'that complex cultural whole'. They were indispensable in maintaining and organizing almost all aspects of the traditional culture, its cognitive, psychological, ideological and social processes. No wonder that every member of the Nenets' traditional society was musically intelligent: everybody received a personal melody-name at birth, learned to create and perform their own songs, and experienced the Beyond during the song performances.

Today, the traditional rituals and customs no longer complement the song performances, whereas the song melodies created by the people still play an important role, unlocking the gates to their mythological world and laying semantic and structural foundations for the still-remembered stories. They remain instrumental in the ecstatic rite technique which the people continue to implement for meaningful purposes, among which is the basic one of survival and adaptation.

Musicologists wonder 'if ... music has any survival value' (Appleton, 1993: 215), and scientists hesitate to answer the question: 'while the survival value or adaptiveness of language ... are evident, ... the function of music within the species remain unclear' (Gardner, 1975: 348). The cultural analysis of the Nenets' song tradition provides a positive answer to this question.

It is well known that many peculiar features of the circumpolar cultures were determined to a great extent by the severe Arctic climate. Indeed, the peoples living in the Arctic land face a multitude of environmental stresses: prolonged cold, extremes of daily and annual photoperiods, 'low supporting biomass', and vitamin deficiency. A monotonous landscape, isolation, and sometimes hunger can lead to extreme physical and psychological exhaustion causing the mental disease known as 'Arctic hysteria'. Biologists claimed that 'the onset of Arctic hysteria was actually triggered by the internal desynchronization of a number of biological rhythms due to the winter darkness' (So, 1980: 74).

Nevertheless, the traditional cultures of the northern people testify to the human adaptability to these conditions. Among the means they utilized to cope with the extremes of climate was the shamanistic technique of ecstasy. The role of ecstasy in the biological and psychological adaptation of the people to the hostile environment was probably the main reason why such altered states of consciousness, considered abnormal in many other societies of the world, were 'socially accepted and specially sought after' in shamanistic culture. Subjective experiences of ecstasy provided a solution of real survival value as they fulfilled many significant goals and needs: the cognitive goal of 'finding a universal and fundamental truth' and the psycho-therapeutic need for relieving anxiety through intense emotion, usually described as catharsis. As this study shows, music has been crucial to the technique of attaining ecstasy, and thus its survival value and role in the people's cultural adaptation can hardly be in doubt.

A concern has recently been expressed against simplistic explanations of the phenomenon of Arctic adaptation governed mainly by ecological and climatological conditions (Krupnik, 1993: 189). Instead, a larger 'adaptation framework' has been rediscovered, which includes other factors involved in cultural dynamics, such as

> population growth, accumulation of hunting knowledge and skills, and intercommunity contact, including exchange of technology as well as environmental change (Krupnik, 1993: 189).

The analyses of the Nenets' song performance practice proves that the musical expression of the people deserves to be included among other factors within the 'adaptation framework'. Various functional parameters of the musical performances satisfy, and at the same time broaden, a number of the criteria defining the phenomenon of Arctic adaptation.

> Adaptation is an active, deliberate adjustment to concrete ecological circumstances in which human beings draw upon and choose from among the technological skills and accomplishments available to them (Krupnik, 1993: 198).

To be able to highlight the crucial role of musical creativity in the survival of this nation, I have had to utilize various analytical methods, such as ethnographic observation, structural analysis of musical texts, and retrospective interpretation of their musical system within its traditional 'mother-culture'. There hardly exists a method which can help us predict a future for the Nenets' song tradition. Nevertheless, it is a legitimate problem to discuss, because 'with every experience in the present we have one eye on the past and the other on the future' (Bruner, 1986: 15). Considering song itself, it is necessary to point out that due to its musical nature, it is well prepared to meet the challenge of new adaptations. The paradigmatic meaning of song melody ensures the possibility of its longevity. Melodic paradigms, capable of adjusting to new contexts and situations, last longer than words. They contain memories of the past while actually living in and coping with the present. Changes in society generate a flux of co-meanings complementing the core traditional meaning of song melody, which can be subjected to a series of social re-comprehensions and semantic reformulations. Nenets song has been through this dynamic before and it could go through it over and over again. Realization of this potential, however, depends on economic and political circumstances.

The situation in the Arctic region today is still unstable and unpredictable. Scholars express different attitudes towards the current economic and political crisis and make contradictory prognoses for the future of the northern minorities and their cultures. Some ethnographers take an active and optimistic position, believing that cooperation with the outside technological world will solve existing problems and serve the interests and rights of the Arctic peoples (Krupnik, 1993: 269). Others do not share this optimistic outlook and believe that the damage which has already been done and continues to be done to the Arctic environment threatens these nations' existence (Oborotova, 1988; Taksami, 1989; Sokolova, 1990a; 1990b; Vakhtin, 1994).

In view of the described conditions, what indeed are the prospects for the survival of Nenets song? Is it going to have some role in a forthcoming 'series of Arctic adaptations'?

Perhaps the economic developments planned for this region can provide some answers to these questions. An 'increasing international interdependence: economical, cultural, political, and ecological' (Hall, 1991: 24) is the factor which is now driving foreign capital into the Arctic region. Although some negative ecological consequences of the industrialization process seem to be inevitable, it may give the northern nations a chance to improve their economic conditions and save their cultural heritage. Such a possibility encourages the view which justifies and promotes cooperation of the native economies with foreign capital.

> On the eve of the twenty-first century, society overall stands faced with the necessity of searching for a new ideology to guide development of polar regions. ... [I]t can never again become a

> region of 'white silence', which will belong only to its ancient inhabitants, returned to some kind of ideally balanced, traditional forms of survival. In the late twentieth century, ... these visions are unrealistic (Krupnik, 1993: 269).

The manifestation of indigenous cultural traditions forms an important part of the investment strategies of the powerful capitalist countries. The new globalization 'cannot proceed without learning to live with and working through differences'. It has a taste for the new exotic and 'a respect for local roots' (Hall, 1991: 31, 35). There is hope that these well-known political motivations will develop favourable conditions for supporting the artistic inspirations of the Nenets people, and give the Nenets' song an opportunity to reach into the future.

Appendix

1.

***Siudbabts* 'Word-Song'**[1]

A small *choom* stood on the bank of the Willow-Bed River.
Word-Song came down inside the *choom* through a chimney.
She saw an old woman taking care of her two children,
a son and a daughter.

From here Word-Song rushed along with the wind.

She saw another *choom*.
Khan Khadengota[2]
lived in that *choom*.
While sleeping Khan Khatengota had a dream:

A small *choom* stood on the bank of the Willow-Bed River.
An old woman lived in that *choom* taking care of her two children,
A son and a daughter.

Khan Khatengota woke up and went out:
'Hey, guys! Drive in my reindeers, I am going for a ride.'
The guys drove in the reindeers, and
Khan Khatengota went to the place he saw in his dream.

He reached the *choom* on the bank of the Willow-Bed River,
Stopped at the door, lifted it and said:
'I could not find you for ten years.
Once, there lived the Owner Iabt Salia.[3]
He was strong.
We, the people from seven lands,
Gathered in the land of Iabt Salia to kill him.
We couldn't kill Iabta Salia for ten years.
After ten years of trying, we killed him.

He was wealthy and had a lot of goods. We shared the goods.
Now I am going to take away his daughter.
In a week I will come back and kill his son.'

He took the girl, threw her on his sledge, and said so:
'The son of the Owner Iabt Salia will stay for a while here.
Next time I will come and kill him.
I need to kill him before he grows up.'
Taking the girl with himself, he went back home.
The girl was crying and crying silently.

From here Word-Song rushed along with the wind.

She flew to the poor small *choom,*
Where an old woman was crying and crying all day long.
The woman said to her son:
'I don't want you to die in front of my eyes, so you'd better go.'
She asked her son to take her coat:
'When it gets cold, cover yourself with it.'
After the boy left, his mother burst out crying.

The boy walked and walked.
In a week he reached a big pasture.
He said to himself: I am very tired, I have to lie down.
He lay down into the hole dug out by a reindeer, and
covered himself with his mother's coat.

From here Word-Song rushed back to Khan Khadengota's choom.

It reached Khan Khadengota's *choom*.
Khan Khadengota said:
'Hey, girl! You are still crying. Probably, you are afraid that
I am going to kill your brother.
Hey, guys, drive in my reindeers.
Whether you want it or not, I am going to kill him.'

The girl went to his reindeers, crying and thinking:
'He is going to kill my mother and brother.'
All of a sudden, she noticed her mother's coat covering a hole in the ground,
and under the coat she found her young brother:
'Why are you here?' When her brother explained why,

she decided: 'Let us die together!'
They began running away.

From here Word-Song flew back to the Khan Khadengota's choom.

Khan Khadengota was asleep.
He woke up, looked into a chimney's hole, and said:
'The girl is absent too long.'
Worrying, he went to check his reindeers.
He did not see the girl anywhere.
Then he found children's footprints, and he said:
She took away her brother, but I won't let them go too far.'
He started tracing the children.

From here Word-Song rushed away along with the wind.

The children were still running and running very fast.
Sometimes, the boy's feet did not touch the ground.
They kept running. Once the girl looked back.
She noticed a man following them.
He was getting closer and closer.
She looked ahead and saw a cape which looked like a sleeve.
They got to the end of the cape and found there an iron sledge
With a stick grown into the ground.
They could hear Khan Khadengota screaming:
'Here, at this cape I killed your father, now I'll kill you too!'
He kept saying: 'I'll kill the boy at the cape of his father!'
The girl thought: 'Indeed, now we are going to die.'
Tears dropped from her eyes.

Khan Khadengota was getting very close.
The girl jumped to the very end of the cape.
From there she looked at the sea. The sea was very big.
The cape formed a deep inlet into the sea.
Ice-floes were slowly moving along the end of the cape.
The girl was standing and thinking.
Then she grabbed a stick,
Tied her brother to her back with a belt, and
Using the stick jumped to the ice-floe.
Jumping from one ice-floe to another,
She moved far away from the cape.

When she reached a very strong ice-floe,
She untied her brother and looked back.
Over there, standing at the end of the cape,
Khan Khadengota was loudly cursing,
Shaking his fists.

Word-Song flew ahead.

The girl and her brother went farther ahead.
There was no land or *choom* around.
Everything looked strange.
They climbed up a big snow hill.
The girl said: Let us take a nap.
We'll start walking again next morning.'
They fell asleep. When they woke up at the dawn
The boy said: 'I am very hungry. I want some meat.'
The girl said: 'I don't have any meat.
Let's go, maybe we'll find other people around.'
The boy began crying and complaining that he was hungry.
The girl said: 'Don't cry, and let's go.'

The whole day they walked and walked until
They reached a big snow hill.
The girl said: 'Let's take a nap until next morning.'
Crying, the boy fell asleep.
The girl does not sleep the whole night thinking:
'How can I feed my brother?'
When the boy woke up at dawn, she told him:
'You sit here. I'll go to find a *choom* and people by myself.'
She walked fast looking around.
All of a sudden, she saw a black dot in the distance.
She started walking faster,
Thinking of her crying brother left behind.

The black dot turned out to be a *choom*.
She went to the *choom* and saw a big pair of skis in front of it.
Silently, she stepped into the *choom*.
There were an old man and an old woman in the *choom*.
A huge man was slumbering in front of a fire.
The old man asked: 'Who came in?'
The old woman said: 'Don't speak. Nobody came in but a dog.'

She took the girl's hand and led her out of the *choom*.
She asked the girl: 'Who are you?'
'Granny, I am looking for some food.
My brother is waiting for me.
He is very hungry, and asks me for some meat.'
The old woman asked again:
'Who are you?'
The girl answered this time:
'My father was the Owner Iabta Salia.'
The old woman said very fast:
'If you are the children of the Owner Iabta Salia, then
Go away immediately.
Khan Khadengota is sleeping in our choom.
He is looking for you.
I will give you some meat, and you should go.'
The old woman gave the girl some meat and fat.
She packed everything and said: 'Now run!'
The girl took everything and rushed back to her brother.

After a while Khan Khadengota woke up and asked:
'Who was in the house?'
The old woman answered:
'A dog came in. I was locking the door.'

Word-Song rushed to the children.

Whirling and spinning she descended on the place
Where the children of the Owner Ibta Salia were resting.

The children were eating. The sister said:
'We can't stay here. Khan Khadengota will be looking for us.
Let's go farther and look for some good people.'
She took her brother's hand and went to the land of strangers.

They walked for a day and another day.
It was getting dark. The girl said:
'Let's take a nap. Next morning we'll start walking again.'
They ate a little bit of meat and fell asleep.
Next morning she said: 'Get up and let's go.'
They walked the whole day and another three days.
They ran out of meat and the boy started crying again.

It was getting dark.
They saw a black dot in the distance.
The black dot turned out to be a big hill.
They climbed and looked down the hill.
They saw a big river and a plane behind it.
There were seven big *chooms* on the plane.
The children went towards the *chooms*.
There was a fire inside the *chooms*.
There were many reindeers near the *chooms*.
They came up closer and closer and crossed the river.
A small creek led to the *chooms*. The girl said:
'You sit here at the creek, while I'll go and look
What kind of people live in the *chooms*.'

The girl approached the *chooms*.
There was a sledge near one of the *chooms*,
She sat on the sledge waiting.
A woman went out of one of the *chooms*,
Carrying a *malitsa*.[4]
She put it on the sledge where the girl was sitting.
She noticed the girl. She said: 'Who are you?
Whose daughter are you, and where did you come from?'
The girl answered:
'I am looking for a fire, food, and good people.
Our father was the Owner Ibta Salia.
My brother is sitting over there. He is hungry.'
She also asked: 'And who are you?'
The woman answered:
'I am a sister of the Seven Sokho.
My seven brothers and Khan Khadengota killed your father.

It is not good for you to be here.
I'd like to help you raise your brother.'

The woman went to another sledge.
She got some reindeer fat, dried meat.
She gave it all to the girl, saying:
'Take it to your brother, and listen to me:
In three days we are going to move from here to another place.
We will return in a year.
In that sledge over there,

You'll find plenty of meat and warm clothes.
After we depart from here,
You and your brother come to this place,
Take the clothes and the food.
Later I will help you again.
When your brother grows up, he'll remember me.
Now you should run back to your brother.
The oldest Sokho is about to wake up. He is very sly.'

The woman went back to her *choom*.
The girl ran back to the creek.
The boy jumped on his feet and asked his sister:
'Did you find some food and good people?'
The girl gave the boy a piece of meat.
They ate together and fell asleep.
At dawn, the girl woke up, looked ahead, and
Saw the Seven Sokho leaving the place.
When the caravan disappeared from her sight,
The girl rejoiced: 'Now we'll be living well.'

The sister and brother were living in a small *choom*.
There was plenty of food and clothes.
They lived a year at the place.
The brother was eating and sleeping in the *choom*.
They lived three years more.
Once the girl looked outside.
In the distance, she saw the caravan of the Seven Sokho
Moving in their direction.
The girl said: 'Let's hide immediately.'

At night, she came back to the *choom* where
She once met the woman who helped them.
The same woman came out of the same *choom*.
She saw the girl and asked: 'How was your life here?'

The girl answered: 'We lived very well.
There was enough food and clothes in the small *choom*.
My brother became a big, strong man.'
The woman said: 'Now I'll help you again.
Tomorrow bring your brother here. I'd like to look at him.'
The girl went back to her brother.

The next day they sat together the whole day
Waiting for the evening to come.
When the evening came there was silence around.
They went along the creek towards the *choom*.
Sister Sokho was there.
She said: 'You, son of the Owner Iabta Salia,
My seven brothers Sokho are very strong.
They helped to kill the Owner Iabta Salia.
My oldest brother has an iron bow.
This bow is your father's bow.
With this bow you'll kill my seven brothers Sokho.
You'll come at night, when they'll be asleep.
Now you go in your *choom*.'
The girl with her brother ran back to their *choom*.

Word-Song stayed with the Sister Sokho.

Sister of the Seven Sokho went to her *choom*.
In the morning her seven brothers went hunting.
For the whole day they were absent.
They came back from hunting late at night.
The oldest brother said:
'Sister, serve us food quickly!
Tomorrow we'll go hunting again.'
They started eating. When they finished they went sleeping.

At midnight, in the dark,
The son of the Owner Iabta Salia
Stopped at the Sokho brothers' *choom* and cried out loudly:
'You, Seven Sokho, do you want to die in your *choom*?'
The Seven Sokho jumped up and took their bows.
The oldest brother said: 'Our sister betrayed us.'
The brothers went out and started shooting.
They were shooting the whole night.
On the one side there were seven brothers Sokho.
On the other side there was one son of the
Owner Iabta Salia.

The son of the Owner Iabta Salia turned out to be stronger.
By the next morning he killed all seven brothers Sokho.
The son of the Owner Iabta Salia said:

'Sister Sokho, you stay with my sister, and
I'll go and find our mother.'
The son of the Owner Iabta Salia left quickly.

Word-Song followed him.

The son of the Owner Iabta Salia reached a small river.
There was a tiny *choom* on the bank of the Willow-Bed River.
He heard his mother crying inside the *choom*:
'Now I am alone. He took my daughter and killed my son.'
Her son silently opened the door and entered the *choom*.
He said: 'Mother, we are alive! I came to take you with us!'
The son of the Owner Iabta Salia took his mother.
They went to the Sokhos' place.
When they reached the place
He gathered a big herd of reindeers. He said:
'Now, you, my sister, sister Sokho, and my mother,
Take the big herd and go to the land of my father.
I am going to find Khan Khadengota.
If I do not come in seven days, I'll be coming in a month.
My sister will show you the way to the land of my father.'
Soon after the son of the Owner of the Iabta Salia left as well.

Word-Song flew after him.

Sooner or later the son of the Owner Iabta Salia
Reached the *choom* of Khan Khadengota.
He cried aloud: 'Khan Khadengota, get out!
I am the son of the Owner Iabta Salia,
Who you killed once.
Now I'll kill you. Let's see who is stronger.'

They were shooting each other the whole day and night.
Then they started wrestling.
The son of the Owner Iabta Salia
Pushed Khan Khadengota on the ground.
Khan Khadengota said: 'I am exhausted.'
The son of the Owner Iabta Salia killed Khan Khadengota, and
He left for his place.

Word-Song flew after him.

The son of the Owner Iabta Salia was riding quite long.
At last a big *choom* appeared at the end of the cape.
This *choom* looked like a big black hill.
There was a big herd of reindeers wandering near the *choom*.
The son of the Owner Iabta Salia reached the *choom*.
He entered the *choom* and said:
'Now there is no death to us!'

The sister of the son of the Owner Iabta Salia said:
'Brother, the sister of the seven Sokho helped us.
She led us to these happy days.
Now you should marry this girl.'
The son of the Owner Iabta Salia said:
'Indeed, I was going to say these words by myself.
You just said them ahead of me.'

The son of the Owner Iabta Salia married
The sister of the Seven Sokho, and
They lived happily ever after on the cape of his fatherland.

2.

***Iarabts* 'Two Seroteta'**[5]

We didn't have many *chooms*,
We had only one hundred *chooms*.
We had twenty thousand reindeers.
I had a sister-in-law.
She was bringing up a boy, maybe her brother.
His name was Khasutsiako At'.[6]
Since I started remembering things
We had been living together for ten years.

My sister-in-law never unloaded our cargo sledge.
I didn't know what was in that sledge.
The things which were in the sledge
Never were put drying under the sun.

Once, my old brother, the older Seroteta,
Started playing with embellishments in

My sister-in-law's braid.
She said: 'Why are you touching my head? It is noisy.
If you want to say a word, say it.'
The older brother said:
'Yes, I have a word. I have a brother. He has grown up.
I want him get married. The Tasinii's have a sister.
The price for her is very high.
All other people are coming back with nothing.
I want to get this woman for my brother.'
My sister-in-law said:
'You seem to be tired living peacefully. You want to die.
You want to leave your blood there.
Many people went to the land of the Tasinii's.
Nobody came back. If you look in our land,
You'll find a woman for him to marry.'
The old brother said:
'I've found you in our land. What else do you want?
I want a woman from a famous clan.'
My sister-in-law became quiet. She said:
'If you want a woman from that land, let us go.
I have a sister there, she is younger than me.'
The old Seroteta said: 'Don't sleep too long.
We are going far away.'

One night passed. We left taking our herd with us.
I am riding four white reindeers.
My sister-in-law bred them.
She fed them with a dog milk from a dog cup.

We had been travelling for a week.

One day, we noticed seven riders on our right.
They were moving towards me. I stopped. They stopped.
Everyone was riding white reindeers. They said:
'You are going to a bad land. You are riding too fast.
Could you give us your reindeers for both riding and eating?'

I said: 'Of course.'
They said: 'When the land won't be peaceful anymore,
We'll come and help you too.
The land of the Tasinii's is bad.

Many people went there. Many of them were killed.'
I went on riding.

We had been travelling for a month.

In a month, I looked to the left.
There was a hundred *chooms* across us.
A man was running from there in our direction.
When he reached us, he asked me,
The one who was urging the reindeers forward.

He was as young as me. He said:
'You, the youngest Seroteta!
When the oldest Seroteta rides reindeer, he rides so fast that
I can't catch him.' I said:
'You obviously know us. But I don't know you.
Who are you?' He said:
'My owners are Seven Pyriatis.
Could you give me a few reindeers for eating?'

I caught a female reindeer and said:
'Take her and tie her up.'
But the female reindeer did not want to go.
He said: 'Why do I need this bony reindeer?
Eat her yourself.' He let her go.
I did not like it. I struck his hand and said:
'You are not smart at all. She did not want to go because
She had to leave her kids behind.
If you had not let her go, I'd give you ten more reindeers.'
The Owned by Pyriati turned his head to my side. He said:

'You, the youngest Seroteta, want to fight with me.
I'll come some day to fight against you.
I'll never forget how you struck my hand.'
And he went back to his *choom*.

We had been travelling for another month.

One day we noticed a rider approaching us from our right.
The rider tried to catch my brother, but he stopped next to me. Snow became red due to the embellishments on the Head of his reindeer.

He was very talkative. He said:
'The youngest Seroteta! You are going to a very bad land.
The seven Tasiniis are my older brothers.
We have one father and two different mothers.
Once, he took my mother as his second wife.
I live separately from my brothers.
I have a sister. She lives with me.
People propose to my sister. Once she gets married,
My brothers kill every husband of my sister.
They ask me to help them, but
I don't want to participate in such a bad thing.
They say that if I don't help them they'll kill me as well.
I left my brothers. I live separately from them.
I couldn't catch your older brother.
Therefore, I am giving my sister to you.
You can marry her. Go with me. I'll give you your wife.'

I said:
'I am not going with you.
My older brother would say later that
While we were travelling I went to a woman.'
He said: 'Then, when you'll be on your way back
Stop by our *choom*.'
He went back the same way he came from.

We had been travelling a week.

In a week, we saw many *chooms*, a hundred *chooms*.
My older brother said:
'We came to the land we wanted to come to.'
We spent a night. In the morning,
My brother and sister-in-law went proposing.
I stayed in our *choom*.

The fire my sister-in-law started yesterday was already out.
I heard the voices of my brother and sister-in-law.
They were singing drunk. They said:
'We have been promised a woman.
The truth is that if you are good,
People are good to you as well.
The seven Tasinii are very good.'

We spent another night.
In the morning, a few riders arrived to get a ransom.
They took a herd of reindeers and ten cargo sledges.
The seven Tasiniis said:
'We took ours. Now come to us for yours.'

There were many of us in the hundred of *chooms*.
We killed a reindeer to eat raw meat.
We started the wedding. The wedding lasted for three days.
After the three days I said to my sister:
'Let's go back to our *choom*. There is no end to this drinking.'

We went back to our *choom*.
Khasutiako At' met us there. He said:
'Where are the rest of your people?
You came back without them.'
I said: 'They stayed there. They are very drunk.
I got tired of that.'

I asked him to kill a reindeer to eat.
We did it. I said to my sister:
'Go and cook this meat for us.'
She went while we started eating raw meat and
Drinking wine from a pot.
I said: 'Khasutiako At'! The Tasiniis will come soon
To propose to my sister. But I'd better give my sister to you.'
We took a sledge. We drove a few circles around.
I gave my sister to Khasutiako At' to marry her.'

Next morning, my brother and sister-in-law
Brought a woman for me. I said:
'I gave my sister in marriage.'
They said: 'You know what you are doing.'
Again they drank for three days.

After the three days, my older brother said:
'We have to go back home.
Otherwise, summer will catch us in the land of strangers.'
I took my woman. We went back home.

After a month of travelling, we decided to stop.

We set up our *chooms*.
My Tasinii woman began cooking.
All of a sudden, she became pale, then red, and pale again.
I said: 'If you want to say something, just say it.'
She said: 'Of course I have a word.
This night let your bow be in your *choom*.
While we were travelling
I saw a little cloud ascending to the sky.
Then I saw a few drops of blood dropped on the ground
Near our sledge.'

I thought: 'Probably, the Owned by Pyriati will come.'
Before falling asleep, I brought my bow into my *choom*.
I just started nodding.
Suddenly, the Owned by Pyriati knocked on my door.
He said: 'You struck me last time.
Now I'll kill you and marry your wife.'

I jumped outside and shouted out:
'You, people in the *chooms*, stay inside. I will kill them myself. There are not many of them.'

I fought with them all night.
I killed all of them. Only the Owned by Pyriati was left alive.
He ran away in an unknown direction.
He said: 'You, the youngest Seroteta!
You did not kill all of our people in the seven lands.
They will come to you eventually.'

We got up the next day, ate, and departed,
Leaving only the dead behind.

Once again, we had been travelling for a month.

The summer came. We stopped and stayed at one place.
I had been sleeping the whole summer,
Never leaving my *choom*.
Then the fall came.
Once, I overheard Khasutiako At' telling the Oldest Seroteta:
'I want to go to my land.'
My brother said: 'If you want, you can go.

You are grown up now.'
Khasutiako At' said: 'From your twenty thousand reindeers
I am going to take a half.'

The Oldest Seroteta said loudly:
'How could you take ten thousand?
There are two of us left here. Those are our reindeers.'
While they were arguing,
Their voices became louder and louder.

I thought: 'I'd rather come out while they are still good.'
I went outside and said:
'The Oldest Seroteta, let us divide the reindeers into two parts.
I will stay reindeerless.'
Khasutiako At' said: 'This is fair.
You did not help me raise and take care of the reindeers.
You were always sleeping while I was taking care of them.'

I said: 'My older brother, let him take those reindeers.'
But my older brother wanted more than a half.
Khasutiako At' said: 'Then I'll take all reindeers and kill you.'

They started wrestling. They fought for three days.
In three days Khasutiako At' put my brother on the ground.
He took out his knife. I thought:
'How can he kill my brother, if my eyes are seeing it?'
I grabbed Khasutialo At' and said:
'You are about to kill a man who brought you up.
He is an old man and you are a young man.'

Khasutiako At' said:
'You want to be stronger than your brother. I'll kill you.'
We started wrestling. We fought for seven days.
Khasutiako At' turned out to be very strong.
When I pushed him he resisted.
When he pushed me I fell down.
In a week, he put me on the ground.
Sitting on my chest, he pulled out a knife. He said:
'Now, two Seroteta, I'll take all of your reindeers,
All your wives, and I'll kill the oldest brother.'

I looked at my *choom*. I thought:
'I have a wife and a sister.
Why don't they come out to help me?'
I told Khasutiako At':
'Take all male reindeers. Leave me only four female ones.'
He did not agree. He said: 'I'd rather kill you.'
I got very angry. I struck him on his chest and said:
'You seem to fight quite seriously. I thought you were joking.'
I jumped on my feet. We began fighting again.

We fought for a week.
A thunder was coming out of our feet.
In a week, I put Khasutiako At' on the ground.
As I was about to pull out my knife,
My sister-in-law showed up.
She said: 'My dearest youngest Seroteta!
Don't kill your comrade.
I brought him up with reindeer and dog milk.'
I said: 'You are sorry for your brother, but
When he tried to kill me, you didn't come to help me.'
My sister showed up. She said:
'My youngest brother! Don't kill your comrade.'
I said: 'When he was sitting on me, you did not come out.
You are sorry for him, but not for me.'
My sister went back to her *choom*.

I looked at my *choom*.
My wife Tasinii came out. She said:
'The youngest Seroteta! Don't kill your comrade.'
I thought: 'Some day I will remind her these words.
Now I'll listen to her.'
I let Khasutiako At' go. I said:
'You can take twenty thousand reindeers.'

I went back to my *choom*.
We lived there for a year.
Nobody left us. Nobody visited us.
I slept all days long.
In a year, I got up.
The woman Tasinii was cooking meat.
All of a sudden, she got pale then red and pale again.

I said: 'You, probably, have a word to say. Say it.'
She said: 'I saw three drops of blood falling on the ground.
I saw a black cloud without an end ascending to the sky.
When I see something like that, bad things happen.
Probably, my seven oldest brothers touched the ground.
My brother is not coming.
Only the sons of the second mother are coming.
I am going to dress you like a female.
I'll hide your oldest brother and sister.
We'll turn our sledges into cargo sledges.
I'll deceive them. They are coming tonight.'

We finished eating. I changed into a female dress.
My wife made and embellished my hair.
I didn't see where she took my sister and brother.
She put me on the bed of my sister.

In the evening our dogs started barking.
Someone striked on my *choom*:
'The youngest Seroteta! Are you going to die in your *choom*?'
The woman Tasinii said:
'The brothers Seroteta are not in the *choom*.
You struck on the *choom* in vain.'

The youngest Tasinii asked loudly:
'Where did they go?'
My wife said: 'A week ago, they left for somewhere.'
He said: 'Don't lie to me.'
She said: 'I am not lying. Look at the sledges.'
He said: 'Yes, there are no sledges around.
Tomorrow we'll go after them.
It is night now.'

My wife asked: 'Did you bring the strongest?' They said:
'We brought Yamal, Tungus, Nganasan, and Piasia.
They are strong.'
We spent the night. In the morning, they said:
'Unset your *chooms*. We are leaving.'

We had been travelling for a week.

I was taken by Tungus and put on his sledge.
He was walking along the sledge very slowly.
I thought: 'Sooner or later, I'd have to kill him anyway.'
I pulled a bow out of the sledge.
I put two arrows on the bow and shot at Tungus.
The arrows didn't get Tungus. He had an iron shirt.
Tungus called for his people. He said to them:
'I am carrying a monster, not a woman.'
I asked my wife to set a *choom*.

A war started.
We fought for a month. Seven Seroteta arrived to help us.
We all shot for a year. Seven Seroteta died.
When only three arrows were left, I said to Tungus:
'Your death has come.' I shot him.
With the second arrow I killed the son of Tungus.
With the third arrow I killed Khasutiako At'. I said:
'I saved you before. I won't do that again.'

We went away. We set up a *choom*.
We took a drum, *pimy*,[7] and *malitsa* into the *choom*.
In this very *choom* we still live.

Notes

1. Recorded by Kupriianova in 1949 in Nel'min Nos from Ie. Taleieva (Kupriianova, 1965: 182-93). English translation from Russian by the author.
2. Literally, sledge with clutches.
3. The owner of the narrow cape.
4. *Malitsa* is a fur coat.
5. Recorded by Kupriianova in 1959 in Nel'min Nos from A. Taleieva (Kupriianova, 1965: 224-38). English translation from Russian by the author.
6. Literally, the young Khasutsiako.
7. *Pimy* are fur boots.

Bibliography

Aaron, S. (1994), 'Intelligence in Traditional Music', in Khalfa, J. (ed.), *What Is Intelligence?*, The Darwin College Lectures, New York, Cambridge University Press.

Abrahams, R. (1975), 'The Theoretical Boundaries of Performance', in Herndon, M. and Brunyate, R. (eds), *Form in Performance, Hard-Core Ethnography*, Texas: The University of Texas.

Abramovich-Gomon, A. (1998), 'Bird Song Research and the Problem of Brain/Culture Correlation', *The Forty-third Annual Meeting of the Society for Ethnomusicology, Abstracts*, Bloomington.

Alekseiev, E. (1973), 'O zvukoriadnykh variantakh traditsionnykh iakutskikh pesen v sviazi s nekotorymi osobennostiami ikh ladovoi organizatsii' [The pitch organization of the traditional Yakut songs], in Zemtsovsky, I. (ed.), *Problemy muzykal'nogo fol'klora narodov SSSR*, Moskva: Muzyka.

Alekseiev, E. (1976), *Problemy formirovaniia lada: na materiale iakutskoi narodnoi pesni* [The problems of mode organization: based on Yakut folk songs], Moskva: Muzyka.

Angere, J. (1956), *Die uralo-jukagirische Frage*, Stockholm: Almqvist and Wiksell.

Anuchin, V. (1914), 'Ocherk shamanstva u ieniseiskikh ostiakov' [A description of shamanism among the Ienisei Ostyaks], *Sbornik Muzeia Antropologii i Etnografii*, vol. 2, no. 2, St Petersburg: Tipografiia Imperatorskoi Akademii Nauk.

Appleton, J. (1993), 'Epilogue. Implications for Contemporary Musical Practice', in Tighe, T. and Dawling, J. (eds) *Psychology and Music*, Hillsdale: Earlbaum Associates.

Bakhtin, M. [Medvedev] (1928), *Formal'nyi metod v literaturovedenii. Kriticheskoe vvedenie v sotsiologicheskuiu poetiki* [The formal method in literary scholarship. Critical introduction to sociological poetics], Leningrad. English translation by Wehrle, A., 1978, Baltimore: Johns Hopkins University.

Bakhtin, M. [Voloshinov] ([1929]; 1972), *Marksizm i filosofiia iazyka. Osnovnyie problemy sotsiologicheskogo metoda v nauke o iazyke.*

[Marxism and the philosophy of language. The basic problems of sociological analysis in the science of language], Series Anastasica, vol. 5, The Hague: Mouton.

Banyai, E. (1984), 'On the Technique of Hypnosis and Ecstasy', in Hoppal, M. (ed.), *Shamanism in Eurasia,* vol. 1, Göttingen: Edition Herodot.

Basilov, V. (1984), 'The Study of Shamanism in Soviet Ethnography', in Hoppal, M. (ed.), *Shamanism in Eurasia,* vol. 1, Göttingen: Edition Herodot.

Bauman, R. (1975), 'Verbal Art as Performance', *American Anthropologist,* vol. 77, no. 2, 290-311.

Becker, J. and Becker, A. (1981), 'A Musical Icon: Power and Meaning in Javanese Gamelan Music', in Steiner, W. (ed.) *The Sign in Music and Literature*, Austin: University of Texas Press.

Behague, G. (1984), 'Introduction' in Behague, G. (ed.), *Performance Practice: Ethnomusicological Perspectives.* Westport: Greenwood Press.

Benjamin, Archimandrite (1858), 'Samoiedy mezen'skiie' [The Mezen' Samoyeds], *Etnograficheskii sbornik,* vol. 4, St Petersburg: Tipografiia Ministerstva Vnutrennikh Del.

Berg, L. (1922; 1969), *Nomogenesis or Evolution Determined by Law,* Cambridge: The MIT Press.

Bogdanov, I. (1978), 'K izucheniiu muzyki narodov Severa SSSR' [Studying the music of the northern peoples of the USSR], in Iefimenkova, B. (ed.), *Traditsionnoie and sovremennoie narodnoie muzykal'noie iskusstivo.* Sbornik trudov Gosudarstvennogo muzykal'no-pedagogicheskogo Instituta im. Gnesinykh, vol. 29, Moskva: GMPI im. Gnesinykh.

Bogdanov, I. (1982), 'O nekotorykh iavleniiakh i zakonomernostiakh sinkretizma fol'klora (na primere muzykal'nogo fol'klora finno-ugrov i narodnostei Severa)' [The phenomenon of syncretism in the musical folklore of Finno-Ugrians and other northern peoples], in Rüütel, and Jarva, I. (eds), *Finno-ugorskii muzyka''nyi fol'klor: problemy sinkretizma,* Tallin: Eesti teaduste akadeemia-keele ja kirjanduse instituut.

Bogoraz-Tan, V. (1904-10), 'The Chuckchee', *Memoires of the American Museum of Natural History*, vol. 11, nos 1-2, New York: American Museum of Natural History.

Bogoraz-Tan, V. (1910), 'K psikhologii shamanstva u narodov Severo-Vostochnoi Azii' [On the psychology of shamanism among the people of north-eastern Asia], *Etnograficheskoie Obzreniie,* vol. 1, no. 2, 1-31.

Bogoraz-Tan, V. (1919), 'O tak-nazyvaiemom iazyke dukhov (shamanskom) u raznykh vetvei eskimoskogo plemeni' [About the language of spirits among the shamans and members of the Eskimo tribe],

Izvestiia Akademii Nauk, vol. 13, nos 8-11, 489-95, Petrograd: Akademiia Nauk.

Bogoraz-Tan, V. (1922), 'O pervobytnykh plemenakh. Nabroski k proektu organizatsii upravleniia pervobytnymi tuzemnymi plemenami' [About the aboriginal tribes. Proposal for governing], *Zhizn' Natsional'nostei*, January 10, n. 1 (130), 1, Moskva: Organ Narodnogo Komissariata po delam natsional'nostei.

Bouda, K. (1940), 'Die finnisch-ugrisch-samojedische Schicht des Jukagirischen', *Ungarische Jahrbucher*, no. 20, 71-93.

Brand, A. (1934), *Songs of Wild Birds*, New York: Cornell University.

Briusov, A. (1952), *Ocherki istorii plemion evropeiskoi chasti SSSR v neoliticheskuiu epokhu*, [Essays on the history of the tribes of the European part of the USSR during the neolithic era], Moskva: Nauka.

Brummett, V. (1997), *Ithaca Conference '96. Music as Intelligence*. Ithaca: Ithaca College.

Bruner, E. (1986), 'Experience and its Expression', in Bruner, E. and Turner, V. (eds), *Anthropology of Experience*, Urbana and Chicago: University of Illinois Press.

Bubrikh, D. (1948), 'K voprosu ob otnosheniiakh mezhdu samoedskimi i finno-ugorskimi iazykami' [The problem of the relationship between Samoyed and Finno-Ugrian Languages], *Izvestiia Akademii Nauk SSSR* , vol. 7, no. 6, 511-17.

Butler, D. (1992), *The Musician's Guide to Perception and Cognition*, New York: Schirmer Books.

Castren, M. (1846), 'Russkiie samoiedy. Iz pisem Kastrena' [The Russian Samoyeds. Excepts from Castren's correspondence], *Sovremennik*, vol. 44, 40-71, St Petersburg: Guttenbergov Tipografiia.

Castren, M. (1856), *Reiseberichte und Brief aus den Jahren 1845-1849*, St Petersburg: Buchdr. der Kaiserlichen Akademie der Wissenschaften.

Castren, M. (1860), 'Puteshestviie Aleksandra Kastrena po Laplandii, Severnoi Rossii i Sibiri: 1838-44, 1845-49' [Travelling in Lapland, North Russia, and Siberia by Alexander Castren: 1838-44, 1845-49], *Magazin zemlevediniia i puteshestvii. Geograficheskii sbornik Nikolaia Frolova*, vol. 6, Moskva: Tipografiia Aleksandra Semiona.

Chadwick, N. and Zhirmunsky, V. (1969), *Oral Epics of Central Asia*, London: Cambridge University Press.

Chernetsov, V. (1935), 'Drevniaia primorskaia kul'tura na poluostrove Yamal' [The ancient maritime culture on the Yamal peninsula], *Sovetskaia etnografiia*, vol. 4, no. 5, 109-33.

Christiansen, R. (1953), 'Ecstasy and Arctic Religion', *Studia Septentrionalia*, vol. 4, no. 1, 19-92, Oslo.

Collinder, B. (1954), 'Proto-Lappisch and Samojed', *Sprakvetenskapliga Sallskapets i Uppsala Forhandlingar*, Uppsala: Almquist and Wiksell.

Cushing, G. (1981), 'Ob-Ugrian', in Hatto, A. (ed.), *Traditions of Heroic and Epic Poetry*, vol. 1, London: The Modern Humanities Research Association.

Cytowic, R. (1989), *Synesthesia: A Union of Senses*, New York: Springer Verlag.

Cytowic, R. (1995), 'Synesthesia: Phenomenology and Neuropsychology. A Review of Current Knowledge', *Psyche: an Interdisciplinary Journal of Research on Consciousness*, vol. 2, no. 10.

Czaplicka, M. (1914), *Aboriginal Siberia, a Study in Social Anthropology by M. A. Czaplicka,* Oxford: Clarendon Press.

Décsy, G. (1966), 'Yurak Chrestomathy', *Uralic and Altaic Series*, vol. 50, Bloomington: Indiana University Publications.

Deely, J. (1986), 'Idolum. Archeology and Ontology of the Iconic Sign', in Bouissac, P., Herzfeld, M., and Posner, R. (eds), *Iconicity*, Stauffenburg Verlag.

Deely, J. (1990), *Basics of Semiotics*, Bloomington: Indiana University Press.

Deikman, A. (1969), 'Deautomatization and the Mystic Experience', in Tart, Ch. (ed.), *Altered States of Consciousness*, New York: John Wiley and Sons.

Dioszegi, V. (1968), 'The Problem of the Ethnic Homogeneity of Tofa (Karagas) Shamanism', in Dioszegi, V. (ed.), *Popular Beliefs and Folklore Tradition in Siberia*, Bloomington: Indiana University Press.

Dioszegi, V. (1978), 'Pre-Islamic Shamanism of the Baraba Turks and some Ethnogenetic Conclusions', in Dioszegi, V. and Hoppal, M. (eds), *Shamanism in Siberia.* Budapest: Akademia Kiado.

Dobrovol'sky, B. (1965), 'O napevakh nenetskikh epicheskikh pesen' [The Nenets epic song melodies], in Kupriianova, Z. (ed.), *Epicheskiie pesni Nentsev*, Moskva: Nauka.

Dolgikh, B. (1952), 'Proiskhozhdeniie nganasanov' [The origin of the Nganasans], *Trudy Instituta Etnografii*, vol. 18, 5-18, Moskva: Isdatel'stvo Akademii Nauk SSSR. Reprinted in Michael, H. (ed.), (1962), *Studies in Siberian Ethnogenesis*, Toronto: University of Toronto Press.

Dolgikh, B. (1960), 'Rodovoi i plemennoi sostav narodov Sibiri v XVII veke' [The clan composition of the Siberian indigenous peoples in the seventeenth century], *Trudy Instituta Etnografii*, vol. 55, Moskva: Izdaniiie Akademii Nauk SSSR.

Dolgikh, B. (1961) *Mifologicheskiie skazki i istoricheskiie predaniia entsev* [The Enets' mythological tales and historical legends], Moskva: Glavnaia Redaktsiia Vostochnoi Literatury.

Dolgikh, B. (1962), 'Rodovaia ekzogamiia u nganasan i entsev' [Clan exogamy among the Nganasans and Enets], *Sibirskii etnograficheskii sbornik*, vol. 4, Moskva: Izdaniie Akademii Nauk SSSR.

Dolgikh, B. (1970a), *Ocherki po etnicheskoi istorii nentsev i entsev* [Essays in the Nenets' and Enets' ethnic history], Moskva: Nauka.

Dolgikh, B. (1970b), *Obshchestvennyi stroi u narodov severnoi Sibiri* [Social organization of the North-Siberian Peoples], Moskva: Nauka.

Dolgikh, B. (1976), *Mifologicheskiie i istoricheskiie predaniia nganasan.* [The Nganasans' mythological tales and historical legends], Moskva: Nauka.

Dolgikh, B. (1978), 'Nganasan Shaman Drums and Costumes', in Dioszegi, V. and Hoppal, M. (eds), *Shamanism in Siberia,* Budapest: Akademia Kiado.

Donner, K. (1926), 'A Samoyede Epic', *Journal de la Societe Finno-Ougrienne,* vol. 30, no. 26, 1-13. Helsinki: Suomalais-Ugrilainen Seuran Aikakauskirja.

Donner, K. (1954), *Among the Samoyed in Siberia,* New Haven: Human Relations Area Files.

Doore, G. (1988), 'Shamans, Yogis, and Bodhisattvas', in Doore, G. (ed.), *Shaman's Path: Healing, Personal Growth, and Empowerment,* Boston: Shambhala.

Drogalina, Zh. and Nalimov, V. (1978), 'Rhythm Semantics: Rhythm as a Direct Entry into a Continuous Flow of Images, in Prangishvili, A. (ed.), *The Unconscious,* vol. 3, Tbilisi: Metsniereba Publishing House.

Dul'zon, A. (1961), 'Dorusskoie naseleniie zapadnoi Sibiri' [Population of the Western Siberia before the arrival of the Russians], in Shunkov, V. (ed.), *Voprosy Istorii Sibiri i Dal'nego Vostoka,* Novosibirsk: Izdatel'stvo Sibirskogo Otdeleniia Akademii Nauk SSSR.

Durkheim, E. ([1915]; 1995), *The Elementary Forms of the Religious Life,* New York: The Free Press.

Dyson-Hudson, R. and Dyson-Hudson, N. (1980), 'Nomadic Pastoralism', *Annual Reviews of Anthropology,* vol. 9, 15-61.

Eco, U. (1976, 1979), *A Theory of Semiotics,* Bloomington: Indiana University Press.

Eco, U. (1990), 'Introduction', in Lotman, Iu., *Universe of the Mind,* Bloomington: Indiana University Press.

Eliade, M. (1964), *Shamanism. Archaic Techniques of Ecstasy,* New York: Pantheon Books.

Emsheimer, E. (1946; 1964), 'Schamanentrommel und Trommelbaum', *Ethnos*, vol. 11, 166-81.

Emsheimer, E. (1970), 'Traditional recitation forms of the epic chants', in Cvetko, D. (ed.), *Reports of the 10th International Musicological Society's Congress*, Ljubljana: University of Ljubljana.

Emsheimer, E. (1991a), 'On the Symbolism of the Lapp Magic Drum', *Studia Ethnomusicologica Eurasiatica*, vol. 2, no. 62, Stockholm: The Royal Swedish Academy of Music.

Emsheimer, E. (1991b), 'On the Ideology, Function, Musical Structure and Style of Performance of Siberian Epics, *Studia Ethnomusicologica Eurasiatica*, vol. 2, no. 62, Stockholm: The Royal Swedish Academy of Music.

Emsheimer, E. (1991c), 'On the Ergology and Symbolism of a Shaman Drum of the Khakass', *Studia Ethnomusicologica Eurasiatica*, vol. 2, no. 62, Stockholm: The Royal Swedish Academy of Music.

Feld, S. (1984), 'Sound Structure as Social Structure', *Ethnomusicology*, vol. 27, no. 3, 383-409.

Fischer, R. (1975), 'Cartography of Inner Space', *Altered States of Consciousness*, Conference sponsored by the Smithsonian Institution and the Drug Abuse Council, Washington: The Drug Abuse Council.

Fisher, I. (1774), *Sibirskaia istoriia* [The Siberian history], St Petersburg: Akademiia Nauk.

Fodor, J. (1983), *The Modularity of Mind*, Cambridge: The MIT Press.

Foss, M. (1952), *Drevneishaia istoriia Severa evropeiskoi chasti SSSR* [The ancient history of the North of the European part of the USSR], Moskva: Izdatel'stvo Akademii nauk SSSR.

Frazer, J. ([1910], 1968), *Totemism and Exogamy*, vols 1-4, London: Dawsons of Pall Mall.

Freud, Z. (1933), *New Introductory Lectures on Psycho-analysis*, New York: Norton.

Frid, G. (1991), 'Yamal – 1938', *Muzykal'naia Zhizn'*, no. 6, 29-31.

Gardner, H. (1975), *The Shattered Mind*, New York: Alfred A. Knopf.

Gardner, H. (1983), *Frames of Mind. The Theory of Multiple Intelligences*, New York: Basic Books, Inc., Publishers.

Gardner, H. (1985), *The Mind's New Science*, New York: Basic Books, Inc., Publishers.

Geertz, C. (1957), 'Ritual and Social Change: a Javanese Example', *American Anthropologist*, vol. 59, no. 1, 32-54.

Geertz, C. (1966), *Person, Time and Conduct in Bali: An Essay in Cultural Analysis*, Yale: Southeast Asia Program.

Geertz, C. (1973), 'Thick Description: Toward an Interpretive Theory of Culture', *The Interpretation of Cultures. Selected Essays,* New York: Basic Books.

Georgi, J. (1777), *Opisaniie vsekh v Rossiiskom gosudarstve obitaiushchikh harodov, takzhe ikh zhiteiskikh obriadov, ver, obyknovenii, zhilishch, odezhd i prochikh dostoprimechatel'nostei,* vol. 3: *Samoiedskiie, mandzhurskiie, and vostochnyie sibirskiie narody* [Description of all the peoples of the Russian empire, and also of their life rituals, beliefs, traditions, dwellings, clothing, and other peculiarities, vol. 3: Samoyed, Manchzhur and Eastern Siberian Peoples], St Petersburg: Tipografiia Artilleriiskogo i Inzhenerno-Shliakhetnogo Kadetskogo Korpusa.

Gilberg, R. (1984), 'How to recognize a shaman among other religious specialists', in Hoppal, M. (ed.), *Shamanism in Eurasia,* vol. 1, Göttingen: Edition Herodot.

Gill, M. (1978), 'Hypnosis as an Altered and Regresses State of Consciousness', in Prangishvili, A. (ed.), *The Unconscious,* vol. 2, Tbilisi: Metsniereba Publishing House.

Gomon, A. (1980), 'O nekotorykh osobennostiakh traditsyonnykh nenetskikh improvizatsii' [Some features of the Nenets' traditional Improvisations], in Rüütel, I. (ed.), *Finno-ugorskii muzyka'nyi fol'klore i vzaimosviazi s sosednimi ku'turami,* Tallin: Eesti Raamat.

Gomon, A. (1990), 'Expanded Melodic Scale in the Oral Tradition of the Nenets Folksong', *Ural-Altaic Yearbook,* vol. 62, 75-87, Bloomington: Eurolingua.

Gomon, A. (1992), 'The Melody-Word Counterpoint and its Textualization', *Ural-Altaic Yearbook,* vol. 64, 35-48, Bloomington: Eurolingua.

Grachiova, G. (1984), 'Shaman Songs and Worldview', in Hoppal, M. (ed.), *Shamanism in Eurasia,* vol. 1, Göttingen: Edition Herodot.

Grigor'ian, G. (1956), 'V Yakutii' [In Yakutiia], *Sovetskaia muzyka,* no. 10, 71-8.

Grigor'ian, G. (1957), 'Muzykal'naia kul'tura Iakutskoi ASSR' [Musical culture of the Yakut Autonomous Republic], in Litinsky G. (ed.), *Muzykal'naia kul'tura avtonomnych respublik RSFSR,* Moskva: Muzgiz.

Hajdu, P. (1950), 'Die Bennennungen der Samojedenvolker', *Journal de la Societie Finno-Ougrienne,* vol. 54, 5-112, Helsinki.

Hajdu, P. (1953), 'K Etnogenezu Vengerskogo Naroda', *Acta Linguistica,* vol. 2, Budapest.

Hajdu, P. (1962), 'Etymologische Bemerkungen', Mémoires de la Société Finno-Ougrienne, vol. 125, 53-7, Helsinki.

Hajdu, P. (1963), 'The Samoyed Peoples and Languages', *Uralo-Altaic Stduies*, vol. 14, Bloomingon: Indiana University Publications.

Hajdu, P. (1968), 'The Classification of Samoyed Shamans', in Dioszegi, V. (ed.), *Popular Beliefs and Folklore Tradition in Siberia*, Bloomington: Indiana University.

Hajdu, P. (1978), 'The Nenets Shaman Song and its Text', in Dioszegi, V. and Hoppal, M. (eds), *Shamanism in Siberia*, Budapest: Akademia Kiado.

Hall, S. (1991), 'The Local and the Global: Globalization and Ethnicity', in King, A. (ed.), *Culture, Globalization and the World-System*, Binghamton: State University of New York.

Hall, C. and Nordby, V. (1978), 'Empirical Evidence for the Timelessness of the Unconscious', in Prangishvili, A. (ed.), *The Unconscious*, vol. 2, Tbilisi: Metsniereba Publishing House.

Hardwick, Ch. (ed.) (1977), *Semiotics and Significs. The Correspondence between Charles S. Peirce and Victoria Lady Welby*, Bloomington and London: Indiana University Press.

Harner, M. (1988), 'What is a Shaman?' in Doore, G. (ed.), *Shaman's Path: Healing, Personal Growth, and Empowerment*, Boston: Shambhala.

Hatto, A. (1970), *Shamanism and Epic Poetry in Northern Asia*, London: University of London.

Hatto, A. (ed.) (1981), *Traditions of Heroic and Epic Poetry*, vol. 1: *The Traditions*, London: The Modern Humanities Research Association.

Hartshorne, Ch. (1972; 1992), *Born to Sing*, Bloomington: Indiana University Press.

Heinze, R-I. (1991), *Shamans of the 20th Century*, New York: Irvington Publishers, Inc.

Herzfeld, M. (1993), 'In Defiance of Destiny: the Management of Time and Gender at a Cretan Funeral', *American Ethnologist*, vol. 20, no. 2, 241-55.

Hodges, D. (ed.) (1996), *Handbook of Music Psychology*, San Antonio: IMR Press.

Hornbostel, von E. (1927), 'The Unity of Senses', *Psyche*, vol.7, no. 28, 83-9.

Houston, J. (1975), 'Exploration and Uses of Altered States of Consciousness', *Altered States of Consciousness*, Conference sponsored by the Smithsonian Institution and the Drug Abuse Council, Washington: The Drug Abuse Council.

Hultkrantz, A. (1978), 'Ecological and Phenomenological Aspects of Shamanism', in Dioszegi, V. and Hoppal, M. (eds), *Shamanism in Siberia*, Budapest: Akademia Kiado.

Hultkrantz, A. (1984), 'Shamanism and Soul Ideology', in Hoppal, M. (ed.), *Shamanism in Eurasia,* vol. 1, Göttingen: Edition Herodot.

Humphrey, G. (1963), *Thinking,* New York: Science Edition.

Huxley, J. (1956), 'Evolution, Cultural and Biological', in Thomas, W. (ed.), *Current Anthropology,* Chicago: The University of Chicago Press.

Hymes, D. (1977), 'Discovering Oral Performance and Measured Verse in American Indian Narrative', *New Literary History,* vol. 8, no. 3, 431-57.

Iakoby, A. (1893), *Ugasaniie inorodcheskikh plemion Severa* [The extinction of the native tribes of the North], St Petersburg: Tipografiia Doma Prezreniia.

Irimoto, T. and Yamado, T. (eds) (1994), *Circumpolar Religion and Ecology,* Tokyo: University of Tokyo Press.

Islavin, V. (1847), *Samoiedy v domashnem i obshchestvennom bytu* [The Samoyeds at daily home and social life], St Petersburg: Tipografiia Ministerstva Gosudarstvennykh Imushchestv.

Ivanov, V. (1974), 'The significance of M.M. Bakhtin's Ideas on Sign, Utterance, and Dialogue for Modern Semiotics', in Baran, H. (ed.), *Semiotics and Structuralism,* White Plains: IASP, Inc.

Jakobson, R. (1960), 'Closing Statement: Linguistic and Poetics'. in Sebeok, Th. (ed.), *Style in Language,* New York: John Wiley and Sons, Inc..

Jakobson, R. (1983), *Dialogues,* Cambridge: The MIT Press.

Janhunen, J. (1986), 'Siberian Shamanistic Terminology', in Lehtinen, I. (ed.), *Traces of the Central Asian Culture in the North,* Helsinki: Soumalais-Ugrilainen Seuran Toimituksia, vol. 194.

Jochel'son, W. (1926), 'The Yukaghir and the Yukaghirized Tungus', in Boas, F. (ed.) *Memoire of the American Museum of Natural History,* vol. 1-3, NY: G.E. Stechert.

Johnstone, B. (1987), 'Perspectives on Repetition. Introducton', *Text,* vol. 7, no. 3, The Hague: Mouton.

Joki, A. (1978), 'Notes on Selkup Shamanism', in Dioszegi, V. and Hoppal, M. (eds), *Shamanism in Siberia,* Budapest: Akademia Kiado.

Jones, M. and Holleran, S. (eds) (1992), *Cognitive Bases of Musical Communication.* Washington, DC: American Psychological Association.

Kenin-Lopsan, M. (1987), *Obriadovaia praktika i fol'klor Tuvinskogo shamanstva, konets 19 -nachalo 20 v.* [Ritual practice and folklore of Tuvin shamanism], Novosibirsk: Nauka.

Key, M. (1963), 'Music of the Siriono (Guaranian)', *Ethnomusicology,* vol. 7, no.1, 17-21.

Khalfa, J. (1994), 'Introduction: What is Intelligence', in Khalfa, J. (ed.), *What is Intelligence?* The Darwin College Lectures, New York.: Cambridge University Press.

Khomich, L. (1966), *Nentsy. Istoriko-etnograficheskiie ocherki* [The Nenets: historical and ethnographic essays], Moskva-Leningrad: Nauka.

Khomich, L. (1978), 'A Classification of Nenets Shamans', in Dioszegi, V. and Hoppal, M. (eds), *Shamanism in Siberia*, Budapest: Akademia Kiado.

Kivy, P. (1993), *The Fine Art of Repetition: Essays in the Philosophy of Music*, Cambridge: Cambridge University Press.

Kodolanyi, J. (1976), 'North Eurasian Hunting, Fishing and Reindeer-breeding Civilizations', in Hajdu, P. (ed.), *Ancient Cultures of the Uralian Peoples*, Budapest: Corvina Press.

Kolycheva, I. (1956), 'Nentsy Ievropeiskoi Rossii v kontse XVII – nachale XVIII v. [The Nenets of the European Russia in the end of the 17th – the beginning of the 18th centuries], *Sovetskaia ethnografiia*, no. 2, 76-88.

Konkka, U. and Gomon, A. (1977), 'Karel'skiie prichitaniia' [Karelian Laments], in Rüütel, I. (ed.), *Soome-ugri rahvaste muusikaparandist*, Tallin: Eesti Raamat.

Kraut, R. (1992), 'On the Possibility of a Determinate Semantics for Music', in Jones, M. and Holleran, S. (eds), *Cognitive Bases of Musical Communication*, Washington, DC: American Psychological Association.

Krupnik, I. (1989), *Arcticheskaia Etnoekologiia* [Arctic ethnoecology], Moskva: Nauka; English translation: (1993), *Arctic Adaptation*, Hanover: Dartmouth College.

Krupnik, I. (1993), *Arctic Adaptation*, Hanover: Dartmouth College.

Kuhn, Th. (1970), *The Structure of Scientific Revolutions*, Chicago: University of Chicago Press.

Kupriianova, Z. (ed.) (1960), *Nenetskii fol'klor* [Nenets Folklore], Leningrad: Uchpedgiz.

Kupriianova, Z. (1965), *Epicheskiie pesni Nentsev* [The Nenets' Epic Songs], Moskva: Nauka.

Lamb, S. (1966), *Outline of Stratificational Grammar*, Washington DC: Georgetown University Press.

Lashook, L. (1958), *Ocherk etnicheskoi istorii Pechorskogo kraia* [An essay on the ethnic history of the Pechora region], Syktyvkar: Komi Knizhnoie Izadetel'stvo.

Lashook, L. (1968), 'Sirtia' – drevniie obitateli Subarctiki' ['Sirtia' – the ancient residents of the sub-Arctic], in Alekseiev, V. and Gurvich, I. (eds), *Problemy antropologii i istoricheskoi etnografii Azii*, Moscow: Nauka.

Lehtisalo, T. (1922), 'Jurakkisamojedien lauluista', *Kalevalaseuran vuosikirja*, vol. 2, 82-102, Helsinki.

Lehtisalo, T. (1940), *Samojedische Volksdichtung*, gesammelt von M. Castren, Helsinki: Mémoires de la Société Finno-Ougrienne, vol. 83.

Lehtisalo, T. (1947), *Juraksamojedische Volksdichtung*, Helsinki: Mémoires de la Société Finno-Ougrienne, vol. 90.

Lehtisalo, T. (1960), *Samojedische Sprachmaterialien*, gesammelt von M. Castren, Helsinki: Mémoires de la Société Finno-Ougrienne, vol. 122.

Levin, M., and Potapov, L. (eds) (1956; 1964), *The Peoples of Siberia*, Chicago: Chicago University Press.

Levi-Strauss, C. (1963), *Totemism*, Boston: Beacon Press.

Levman, B. (1992), 'The Genesis of Music and Language', *Ethnomusicology*, vol. 36, no. 2, 147-70.

Lewis, I. (1984), 'What is shaman?', in Hoppal, M. (ed.), *Shamanism in Eurasia*, vol. 1, Göttingen: Edition Herodot.

Lord, A. (1960), *The Singer of Tales*, Cambridge: Harvard University Press.

Lotman, Yu. (1970), *Struktura khudozhestvennogo teksta*, Moskva: Iskusstvo; English translation: (1977), *The Structure of the Artistic Text*, Ann Arbor: University of Michigan.

Lowie, R. (1934), *An Introduction to Cultural Anthropology*, New York: Farrar and Reinehart, Inc.

Ludwig, A. (1969), 'Altered States of Consciousness', in Tart, Ch. (ed.), *Altered States of Consciousness*, New York: John Wiley and Sons, Inc.

Marler, P. (1977), 'The Evolution of Communication', in Sebeok, Th. (ed.), *How Animals Communicate*, Bloomington: Indiana University Press.

Maruszewski, M. (1975), *Language Communication and the Brain*, The Hague: Mouton.

Merriam, A. (1964), *The Anthropology of Music*, Evanston: Northwestern University Press.

Meyer, L. (1998), 'A Universe of Universals', *The Journal of Musicology*, vol. 16, no. 1, 3-15.

Miller, G. (1937), *Istoriia Sibiri* [The history of Siberia], Moskva-Leningrad: Akademiia Nauk SSSR.

Mueller, J. (1963), 'A Sociological Approach to Musical Behavior', *Ethnomusicology*, vol. 7, no. 3, 216-20.

Murdock, G. (1967), *Ethnographic Atlas*, Pittsburg: Pittsburg University Press.

Nettl, B. (1983), *The Study of Ethnomusicology*, Urbana: University of Illinois Press.

Nettl, B. (1989), *Blackfoot Musical Thought. Comparative Perspectives*, Kent: Kent University Press.

Nettl, B. (1987; 1992), *The Radif of Persian Music*, Champaign: Elephant and Cat.

Nettl, B. (1994), 'Musical Thinking' and 'Thinking About Music', in Ethnomusicology: An Essay of Personal Interpretation', *The Journal of Aesthetics and Art Criticism*, vol. 52, no. 1, 139-48.

Niemi, J. (1992), *Nenetsien musiikkikulttuuri: laulut ja soittimet* [The musical culture of the Nenets: songs and musical instruments], unpublished master's thesis, Department of Folk Tradition, Tampere: University of Tampere.

Niemi, J. (1998), *The Nenets Songs, A Structural Analysis of Text and Melody*, Tampere: Acta Universitatis Tamperensis 591.

Nordland, O. (1963), 'Shamanism as an Experiencing of 'the Unreal', in Edsman, C. (ed.), *Studies in Shamanism*, Stockholm: Almqvist and Wiksell.

Nöth, W. (1990), *Handbook of Semiotics*, Bloomington and Indianapolis: Indiana University Press.

Novik, Ie. (1984), *Obriad i fol'klor v sibirskom shamanizme: Opyt sopostavleniia struktur* [Ritual and folklore in Siberian shamanism: experiment in a comparison of structures], Moskva: Nauka.

Novik, Ie. (1990), 'Ritual and Folklore in Siberian Shamanism: Experiment in a Comparison of Structures', in Balzer, M. (ed.), *Shamanism: Soviet Studies of Traditional Religions of Siberia and Central Asia*, Armonk: M. E. Sharpe.

Oborotova, Ie. (1988), 'Narody Severa v sovremennom mire: vzgliady i pozitsii.' [The peoples of the North in the modern world: perspectives and viewpoints], *Sovetskaia etnografiia*, no. 5, 146-9.

Okladnikov, A. (1957), 'Iz istorii etnicheskikh i kul'turnykh sviazei neoliticheskikh plemion Srednego Yeniseia' [From the history of ethnic and cultural connections between neolithic tribes of the middle Yenisei], *Sovetskaia arkheologiia*, no. 1, 26-55.

Orenstein, G. (1993), 'Toward an Ecofeminist Ethic of Shamanism and the Sacred' in Adams, C. (ed.), *Ecofeminism and the Sacred*, New York: Continuum.

Ornstein, R. (1972), *The Psychology of Consciousness*, San Francisco: W.H. Freeman and Company.

Pahnke, W. and Richards, W. (1969), 'Implications of LSD and Experimental Mysticism', in Tart, Ch. (ed.), *Altered States of Consciousness*, New York: John Wiley and Sons, Inc.

Pietsch, P. (1981), *Shufflebrain*, Boston: Houghton Mifflin Company.

Peirce, Ch. (1931-35) *Collected Papers*, vols. 1-6, Hartshorne, Ch. and Weiss, P. (eds), Cambridge University Press.

Peirce, Ch. (1958), *Collected Papers*, vols 7-8, Burks, A. (ed.), Cambridge: Harvard University Press.

Popov, A. (1932), *Materialy dlia bibliografii russkoi literatury po izucheniiu shamanstava* [Bibliography of Russian literature on shamanism], Leningrad: Izadetel'stvo Instituta Narodov Severa.

Popov, A. (1944), 'Ieniseiskiie nentsy' [The Yenisei Nenets], *Izvestiia Vsesoiuznogo Geograficheskogo Obshchestva,* vol. 76, no. 2-3.

Porter, J. (1976), 'Jeannie Robertson's *My Son David.* A conceptual Performance Model', *Journal of American Folklore,* vol. 89, no. 89, 7-26.

Posner, M. (ed.) (1989), 'Preface: Learning Cognitive Science', *Foundations of Cognitive Science*, Cambridge: The MIT Press.

Potapov, L. (1970), 'K semantike nazvanii shamanskikh bubnov u narodnostei Altaia' [Semantics of the names of shamanic drums among the Altaic peoples], *Sovetskoie tiurkovedeniie*, no. 3, 86-93.

Potapov, L. (1978), 'The Shaman Drum as a Source of Ethnographical History', in Dioszegi, V. and Hoppal, M. (eds), *Shamanism in Siberia,* Budapest: Akademia Kiado.

Pribram, K. (1971), *Languages of the Brain*, Englewood Cliffs: Prentice-Hall.

Pribram, K. (1978), 'Conscious and Unconscious Processes: A Neurophysiological and Neuropsychological Analysis', in Prangishvili, A. (ed.), *The Unconscious*, vol. 1, Tbilisi: Metsniereba Publishing House.

Prokof'iev, G. (1940), 'Etnogoniia narodnostei Ob'-Yeniseiskogo basseina' [The etnogony of the population of the Ob'-Yenisei basin], *Sovetskaia etnografiia,* no. 3, 67-76.

Prokof'ieva, Ie. (1956) 'Nentsy', in Levin, M. and Potapov, L. (eds), *Narody Sibiri* (The Peoples of Siberia], Moskva: Izdatel'stvo Akademii Nauk SSSR.

Prokof'ieva, Ie. (1961), 'Shamanskiie bubny' [Shamanic Drums], in Levin, M. and Potapov, L. (eds), *Istoriko-etnograficheskii atlas Sibiri* [Historical-Ethnographic Atlas of Siberia], Moskva: Izdatel'stvo Akademii Nauk SSSR.

Pushkariova, Ie. (1990a), 'Lichnyiie pesni Nentsev' [The Nenets' Personal Songs], in Fishman, O., Riabinin, Ye., and Dubov, I. (eds), *Sovremennoie Finno-Ugrovedeniie. Opyt i problemy*, Leningrad: Muzei Etnografii Narodov SSSR.

Pushkariova, Ie. (1990b), 'Nenets Names', *Traditional Folk Belief Today,* Conference dedicated to the 90th anniversary of Oskar Loorits, Tartu: Estonian Academy of Science.

Quine, W. (1960), *Word as an Object*, Cambridge: Technology Press of the MIT.

Radcliffe-Brown, A. (1973), 'On the Concept of Function in Social Science', in Bohannan, P. and Glazer, M. (eds), *Highpoints in Anthropology*, New York: Alfred A.Knopf.

Raffman, D. (1992), 'Proposal for a Musical Semantics', in Jones, M. and Holleran, S. (eds), *Cognitive Bases of Musical Communication*, Washington, DC: American Psychological Association.

Raffman, D. (1993), *Language, Music, and Mind*, Cambridge: The MIT Press.

Rasmussen, K. (1929), 'Intellectual Culture of the Iglulik Eskimos', *Report of the 5th Thule Expedition*, vol. 7, no. 2.

Revunenkova, Ie. (1980), *Narody Malajzii i Zapadnoj Indonezii* [The peoples of Malaysia and Western Indonesia], Moskva: Nauka.

Revunenkova, Ie. (1984), 'O nekotorykh istokakh poeticheskogo tvorchestva v Indonezii (shaman-pevets-skazitel')' [Some Sources of Poetic Creativity in Indonesia: Shaman-Singer-Narrator], in Putilov, B. (ed.), *Fol'klor i etnografiia*, Leningrad: Nauka.

Remezov, S. (1882), *Chertyiozhnaia kniga Sibiri, sostavlennaia v 1701 godu* [A map book of Siberia, prepared in 1701], St Petersburg: Arkheograficheskaia Komissiia.

Ripinsky-Naxon, M. (1993), *The Nature of Shamanism*, Albany: State University of New York Press.

Rivers, W. (1914), *The History of Melanesian Society*, 2 vols, Cambridge: Cambridge University Press.

Rouget, G. (1980), *Music and Trance*, Chicago: The University of Chicago Press.

Saifutdinova, A. (1998), 'O vzaimodeistvii vokal'nogo i instrumental'nogo v nenetskoi traditsionnoi muzykal'noi kul'ture', in Timosjenko, A. (ed.), *Instrumentovedeniie: Molodaia nauka* [Organology: a young science], Conference Abstracts, St Petersburg: Rossiiskii institut istorii iskusstv.

Santos-Granero, F. (1991), *The Power of Love: the Moral Use of Knowledge amongst the Amuesha of Central Peru*, London: The Athlone Press.

Saussure, F. ([1916]; 1964), *Cours de linguistique generale*, Paris: Edition Payot.

Saussure, F. (1986), *Course in General Linguistics*, La Salle: Open Court.

Sebeok, Th. (1968), 'Zoosemiotic Components of Human Communication', in Sebeok, Th. (ed.), *How Animals Communicate*, Bloomington: Indiana University Press.

Sebeok, Th. (1972), *Perspectives in Zoosemiotics*, The Hague: Mouton.

Sebeok, Th. (1976), 'Iconicity', *Modern Language Notes*, no. 91, 1427-56.

Sebeok, Th. (ed.) (1977), *A Perfusion of Signs*, Bloomington: Indiana University Press.

Sebeok, Th. (ed.) (1986), *Encyclopedic Dictionary of Semiotics*, vol. 2, Berlin: Mouton.

Seeger, A. (1980), 'Sing For Your Sister. The Structure and Performance of Suya Akia', in McLeod, N. and Herndon, M. (eds), *The Ethnography of Musical Performance*, PA: Norwood Editions.

Serafine, M. (1988), *Music as Cognition: the Development of Thought in Sound*, New York: Columbia University Press.

Shcherbakova, A. (1960), *Nenetia' vadako'* (The Nenets' Tales), Leningrad: Uchpedgiz.

Sheikin, Yu. (1996), *Muzykal'naia Kul'tura Narodov Severnoi Azii*, Yakutsk: Ministerstvo Kul'tury Respubliki Sakha.

Shirokogoroff, S. (1935), *Psychomental Complex of the Tungus*, London: Kegan, Paul, Trench, Trubner.

Siikala, A-L. (1978), *The Rite Technique of the Siberian Shaman*, Helsinki: Folklore Fellow Communication, vol. 220.

Simon, H. and Kaplan, C. (1989), 'Foundations of Cognitive Science', in Posner, M. (ed.), *Foundations of Cognitive Science*, Cambridge: The MIT Press.

Singer, M. (1972), *When a Great Tradition Modernizes*, New York: Praeger.

Skanke, J. (1943), 'Epitomes Historiae Missionis Lapponicae', in Falkenberg (ed.), *Nordnorske Samlinger*, vol. 5, 1, Oslo: A. W. Broggers.

Smith, W. (1977), 'Communication in birds', in Sebeok, Th. (ed.), *How Animals Communicate*, Bloomington: Indiana University Press.

Snowdon, Ch. and Hausberger, M. (eds) (1997), *Social Influences on Vocal Development*, Cambridge, UK: Cambridge University Press.

So, J. (1980), 'Human Biological Adaptation to Arctic and Subarctic Zones', *Annual Review of Anthropology*, no. 9, 63-82.

Sokolova, Z. (1990a), 'S'iezd malochislennykh narodov Severa (vzgliad etnografa)' [The Congress of the Northern Minorities: an ethnographer's perspective], *Sovetskaia etnografiia*, no. 5, 142-6.

Sokolova, Z. (1990b), Narody Severa SSSR: proshloie, nastoiashcheie i budushcheie' [Peoples of the Far North of the USSR: Their Past, Present, and Future], *Sovetskaia etnografiia*, no. 6, 17-32.

Sorokina, I. (1990), 'Sostoianiie i perspektivy issledovaniia samodiiskikh iazykov' [The State of the Research on Samoyed Languages], *Sovremennoie finno-ugrovedeniie. Opyt i Problemy*, Leningrad: Muzei Etnografii Narodov SSSR.

Spector, M. (1994), 'Arctic Tribe's Hard Life Unchanged for Centuries', *The New York Times*, November 22, p. B7.

Stepanova, A, and Koski, T. (1977), 'Karel'skiie ioigi', in Rüütel, I. (ed.), *Soomme-ugri rahvaste muusikaparandist*, Tallin: Eesti Raamat.

Sternberg, R. (1986), 'A Framework for Understanding Conceptions of Intelligence', in Sternberg, R. and Detterman, D. (eds), *What is Intelligence?*, Norwood: Ablex Publishing Corporation.

Strahlenberg, Ph. (1730), *Der Nord- und Ostliche Theil von Europa und Asia*, Stockholm: Verlegung des Autoris.

Susoi, Ie. (1986), 'Obychai i Traditsyi Nentsev' [Customs and Traditions of the Nenets], *Kul'tura Narodnostei Severa: Traditsyi i Sovremennost'*, Novosibirsk: Nauka.

Svetozarova, N. (1982), *Intonatsionnaia Sistema Russkogo Iazyka* [The intonational system of Russian language], Leningrad: Leningrad University.

Swienko, H. (1978), 'Studia nad szamanizmem [ludow Syberii]. Bibliografia wa prac Polakow oraz prac wydanych w Polsce w latach 1754-1983', in Euhemer, *Przeglad religioznawczy*, no. 3, 163-185, Warszawa: Panstwowe Wydawnictwo Naukowe Problem.

Taksami, A. (1984), 'Survivals of Early Forms of Religion in Siberia', in Hoppal, M. (ed.), *Shamanism in Eurasia*, vol. 2, Göttingen: Edition Heordot.

Taksami, Ch. (1989), 'Gumanitarnyie problemy Severa' [The humanitarian problems of the North], *Sovetskaia etnografiia*, no. 6, 17-29.

Tampere, H. (1983), *Estonskaia narodnaia pesnia* [The Estonian folk song], Leningrad: Muzyka.

Tart, Ch. (1969), 'Introduction', in Tart, Ch. (ed.), *Altered States of Consciousness*, New York: John Wiley and Sons, Inc.

Tedlock, D. (1990), 'From Voice and Ear to Hand and Eye', *Journal of American Folklore*, vol. 103, no. 408, 133-56.

Tereshchenko, N. and Pyrerka, A. (1949), *Neko khadakenda vadako'* [The tales of a woman named Neko], Leningrad: Uchpedgiz.

Tereshcsenko, N. (1954), *Nenetsia' vadako* [Nenets fairy tales], Leningrad: Uchpedgiz.

Tereshchenko, N. (1960), 'A nyenyec nemzetségnevekrõl [On Nenets clan names], in Sándor Mikesy and Dezsõ Pais (eds.), *Névtudományi vizsgalatok*, Budapest: Akademia Kiado.

Tereshchenko, N. (1980), 'O nekotorykh osobennostiakh yazyka fol'klora nentsev' [Some characteristics of the Nenets' folklore language], *Sovetskoie finno-ugrovedeniie*, vol. 1, 41-6, Tallin.

Tereshchenko, N. (1990), *Nenetskii epos* [The Nenets Epic], Leningrad: Nauka.

Tereshchenko, N. (1992), 'Dmitry Vladimirovich Bubrikh o sviaziakh mezhdu samodiiskimi i finno-ugorskimi iazykami' [Dmitry Vladimirovich Bubrikh about the connections between the Samoyed and Finno-Ugrian languages] in Kert, G. (ed.) *D.V. Bubrikh. K stoletiiu so dnia rozhdeniia* [D.V. Bubrikh. On his 100th anniversary], St Petersburg: Nauka.

Thomas, N. and Humphrey, C. (eds) (1994), *Shamanism, History, and the State,* Ann Arbor: The University of Michigan Press.

Toivonen, J. (1950), 'Zur Problem des Protolappischen', *Sitzungsberichte der finnischen Akademic der Wissenschaften,* Helsinki: Verlag.

Tonkov, V. (1936), *Nenetskiie skazki,* [The Nenets Tales], Arkhangel'sk: Sevkraigiz.

Traugott, N. (1978), 'On the Problem of the Unconscious in Neurophysiological Investigations', in Prangishvili, A. (ed.), *The Unconscious*, vol. 1, Tbilisi: Metsniereba Publishing House.

Trevarthen, C. (1990), 'Signs Before Speech', in Sebeok, Th, and Umiker-Sebeok, J. (eds), *Semiotic Web 1989,* The Hague: Mouton.

Turino, Th. (1989), 'The Coherence of Social Style and Musical Creation Among the Aymara in Southern Peru', *Ethnomusicology*, vol. 33, no. 1, 1-30.

Turino, Th. (1990), 'Structure, Content, and Strategy in Musical Ethnography', *Ethnomusicology*, vol. 34, no. 3, 399-412.

Tyler, S. (ed.) (1969), *Cognitive Anthropology*, New York: Tulane University.

Tylor, E. ([1871]; 1958), *Primitive Culture*, vol. 1 and 2, NY: Harper.

Vainshtein, S. (1986), 'Origin of Reindeer-Herding in Eurasia', in Lehtinen, I. (ed.), *Traces of the Central Asian Culture in the North*, Helsinki: Suomalais-Ugrilaisen Seuran Toimituksian, vol. 194.

Väisänen, A. (1948), *Mordwinische Melodien*, Helsinki: Suomalais-ugrilaisen seuran toimituksia, vol. 92.

Väisänen, A. (1965), *Jurak-Samojedische Melodien*, Helsinki: Suomalais-Ugrilaisen Seuran Toimituksia, vol. 136.

Vakhitova, N. (1989), 'Opyt Etnomuzykovedcheskoi Segmentatsii Nenetskikh Napevov' [An ethnomusicological segmentation of Nenets melodies], in Sheikin, Yu. (ed.) *Muzykal'naia Etnografiia Severnoi Azii*, vol. 10, 141-50, Novosibirsk: Sibirskoie Otdeleniie AN SSSR.

Vakhtin, N. (1994), 'Native Peoples of the Russian Far North', in Minority Right Group (ed.), *Polar Peoples*, United Kingdom: Minority Rights Publications.

Vasil'iev, V. (1970), 'Siirtia – legenda ili real'nost' [Siirtia: a Legend or Reality], *Sovetskaia etnografiia*, no. 1, 151-7.

Vasil'iev, V. (1978), Animistic Notions of the Enets and the Yenisei Nenets', in Dioszegi, V. and Hoppal, M. (eds), *Shamanism in Siberia*, Budapest: Akademiai Kiado.

Vasilevich, G. and Levin, M. (1951), 'Tipy olenevodstva i ich proischozhdeniie' [Patterns of reindeer breeding and their origin], *Sovetskaia etnografiia*, no. 1, 63-87.

Vasilevich, G. (1959), 'Ranniie predstavleniia o mire u evenkov' [Early views about the world among the Evenkis], in Tokarev, S. and Chernetsov, V. (eds), *Issledovaniia i materialy po voprosam pervobytnykh religioznykh verovanii*, Moskva: Izdatel'stvo Akademii Nauk SSSR.

Verbov, G. (1936), 'Lesnyie nentsy' [The Forest Nenets], *Sovetskaia etnografiia*, no. 2, 57-70.

Verbov, G. (1937), *Nenetskiie skazki i byliny* [The Nenets tales and epic songs], Salekhard: Yamalo-Nenetskii okruzhnoi komitet novogo alfavita.

Verbov, G. (1939), 'Perezhitki rodovogo stroia u nentsev' [Survivals of the clan society among the Nenets], *Sovestkaia etnografiia*, no. 2, 43-66.

Verbov, G. (1973), 'Dialekt lesnykh nentsev' [The dialect of the Forest Nenets], *Samodiiskii sbornik*, Novosibirsk: Akademii Nauk SSSR.

Voigt, V. (1978), 'Shamanism in North Eurasia as a Scope of Ethnology', in Dioszegi, V. and Hoppal, M. (eds), *Shamanism in Siberia*, Budapest: Akademia Kiado.

Wallin, N. (1991), *Biomusicology. Neurophysiological, Neuropsychological, and Evolutionary Perspectives on the Origins and Purposes of Music*, Stuyvesant: Pendragon Press.

Walsh, R. (1990), *The Spirits of Shamanism*, Los Angeles: Jeremy E. Tarcher, Inc.

Waugh, L. and Monville-Burston, M. (eds) (1990), *Roman Jakobson on Language*, Cambridge: Harvard University Press.

Waugh, L. (1992), 'Let's Take the Con out of Iconicity in the Lexicon', *The American Journal of Semiotics*, vol. 9, no. 1, 7-47.

Wilson, E. (1998), *Consilience. The Unity of Knowledge*, New York: Alfred A. Knopf.

Zhinkin, N. (1965), 'Chetyre kommunikativnyiie sistemy i chetyre iazyka' [Four communicative systems and four languages], Zvegintsev, V. (ed.), *Teoreticheskiie problemy prikladnoi lingvistiki*, Moskva: Izdatel'stvo Moskovskogo Universiteta.

Zhirmunsky, V. (1964), 'Ritmiko-sintaksichaeskii parallelism kak osnova drevne-tiurkskogo narodnogo epicheskogo stikha' [Rhythmic-syntactic parallelism as a foundation of the ancient Turkish epic versification], *Voprosy iazykoznaniia*, vol. 4, 3-24.

Zhirmunsky, V. (1975), *Teoriia stikha* [Theory of versification], Leningrad: Sovetskii Pisatel'.

Zhirmunsky, V. (1979), 'Legenda o prizvanii pevtsa' [A legend about shamanic call], *Sravnitel'noie literaturovedeniie. Vostok i Zapad*. Selective Writings [Comparative philology. East and West. Izbrannyie Trudy], Leningrad: Nauka.

Zhornitskaia, M. (1983), *Narodnoie Khoreographicheskoie Iskusstvo Korennogo Naseleniia Severo-Vostoka Sibiri* [The folk choreographic art of the aboriginal peoples of the north-eastern Siberia], Moskva: Nauka.

Index